Historic English Inns

Historic English Inns

A. W. Coysh

David & Charles : Newton Abbot

ISBN 0 7153 5537 6

Set in 10 on 12pt Times Roman
and printed in Great Britain
by Bristol Typesetting Co Ltd
for David & Charles (Publishers) Limited
South Devon House Newton Abbot Devon

Contents

List of Illustrations

PLATES

The photographs not otherwise acknowledged are reproduced by permission of Trust House Hotels Ltd

IN TEXT

The above drawings are taken from *History of Signboards* by Jacob Larwood and J. C. Hotten, published in 1866

Introduction

The inn has played a significant part in English history. It has been a place where men have met to exchange news, to discuss their problems, to conduct business and to enjoy the company of friends. Whether it is known as an inn, an alehouse, a tavern or, more recently, as a hotel or public house, matters little; the distinctions have always been blurred, never more so than today. In this book the word 'inn' is regarded as all-embracing. It deals exclusively with the architecture, history and literary associations of our inns for there are already many guides available for those who are primarily concerned about the facilities they provide.

The selection of inns has, inevitably, been a personal one but an attempt has been made to present a fair cross section from the humble public house to the 'grand' hotel and to cover a wide geographical field. Happily, there has been a renaissance of the English inn since World War II. They are fewer and better and some owners have shown a real concern to conserve the traditions of the past while catering for the needs of the present.

Most people enjoy using old inns simply because they feel a vague sense of history. The pleasure can be greatly enhanced if the real facts are known. It adds something to a visit to know, as you park your car in a cobbled yard, that strolling players once performed Elizabethan dramas within its confines, or that you are drinking where Tom Paine formed the Headstrong Club, dining in the brewhouse of an ancient abbey, or sleeping, perhaps, where Charles Dickens worked over the plot of a novel, or where the friends of Charles II made plans for his escape to France. It is good to know these things and if we bring an all round connoisseurship to the way we use our inns their best traditions will be preserved for future generations to enjoy.

The Inn in English Life

Many of our inns date back to medieval times. In those days travelling was hazardous; there were few roads worthy of the name and therefore few vehicles. Well-to-do travellers went on horseback, goods were carried by packhorse, and the poor, if they travelled at all, had to do so on foot. The people who did travel were mainly soldiers, merchants, or pilgrims anxious to visit the shrine of some saint, often in the hope that they might be cured of some sickness or disability. There were no inns as we know them today, but after the Norman Conquest every monastery founded a *hospitium* or hospice where callers could ask for a meal and to stay overnight. The monasteries had a Rule of Hospitality which laid down that all who called at the gate should be received and cared for. No traveller was turned away. Those who could afford it would sometimes contribute to the maintenance of the hospice. There was usually a special hospice for the poor, often outside the monastery gates, as in the case of the Pilgrim's Rest at Battle in Sussex. Here food was served on a wooden plank or board on trestles and pilgrims would sleep on a bed of rushes on the floor—they were literally given 'board and lodging'.

Many shrines attracted pilgrims, particularly in the south of England. Canterbury was always pre-eminent and after the murder of Becket in 1170 pilgrims flocked there in large numbers. Others were attracted to the shrine of Edward the Confessor at Westminster Abbey, to Christchurch Priory, famed for its miraculous beam, to the shrine of St Swithun at Winchester, the Chapel of St Joseph of Arimathea at Glastonbury, and to Chichester, Rochester, Salisbury or Gloucester. So many pilgrims came to the shrine of Edward II at Gloucester after his barbarous murder at Berkeley Castle in 1327 that a new hospice had to be built to accommodate them—now the New Inn.

Wealthier pilgrims sometimes went to Rome or to the Holy Sepulchre in Jerusalem, embarking at Dover or Southampton on journeys which might take many months. Special guest-houses were established in these ports where the pilgrims could wait for a good passage. Maison Dieu at Dover, restored in the 1860s and now in use as a civic building, was built by Hubert de Burgh in the reign of Richard II to serve pilgrims bound for Europe. The monks found such a house a serious drain on their resources for some of the wealthy lords expected high standards and in rough weather often stayed for days. Gervaise le Riche founded a God's House in Southampton in 1185 for pilgrims landing at the port on their way to Winchester or Canterbury. The pilgrimages reached their peak in the thirteenth and fourteenth centuries and continued into the fifteenth though there was a decline in the number of pilgrims after the Great Pestilence of 1348-9 which wiped out whole sections of the population.

Two crusading military orders were recognised as the guardians of the pilgrims and other travellers, and also of the sick and destitute. These were the Knights Hospitallers of the Order of St John of Jerusalem and the Knights Templars of Malta. Both adopted an eight-pointed cross as their emblem and this later became one of the earliest inn signs. These orders established commanderies or preceptories, some of them small manor houses, where they worked under strict monastic rules. The mediaeval hospital of St Cross at Winchester, established by Bishop Henry de Blois in the twelfth century, was placed in the care of the Knights Hospitallers and continues some of its traditions today. Many inn signs have their origin in the religious hospices of the past. The Salutation, and The Angel for example derive from the Salutation of the Virgin Mary by the Angel Gabriel.

It must not be thought that the Church alone catered for travellers. Many places had no hospice and the taverns and ale-houses were able to some extent to meet the needs of wayfarers though accommodation was often poor.

The Dissolution of the Monasteries in 1536 brought a great change. The hospices began to disappear and their functions had to be taken over by others, usually the local lord of the manor or 'landlord'. (To this day an innkeeper is often referred to as 'the landlord' even though he may be a tenant.) Fortunately a few of the old guesthouses have survived as buildings—notably the **George and Pilgrims** at Glastonbury in Somerset and the **Angel and Royal** at Grantham in Lincolnshire. Many other inns incorporate parts of the old religious hospices.

By about 1590 the hospices had gone and innkeeping became a private enterprise. Wealthy travellers would put up at the manor house and increasing numbers of taverns and alehouses began to receive travellers. This was a period when larger manor houses were being built and the lord would sometimes turn the smaller house he had vacated into an inn and put it in charge of a servant. Sometimes the lord of the manor erected a special building as an inn. **The Spread Eagle** at Midhurst in Sussex is a good example of a manorial inn.

The Elizabethans were great travellers, stimulated no doubt by the example of their sovereign who sometimes stayed at inns—**The George** at Cranbrook in Kent, for example. Towards the end of the sixteenth century many new inns were built. Some of these had large courtyards surrounded by galleries with bedrooms. A gallery also formed a vantage point for patrons watching a theatrical performance by strolling players in the courtyard below. **The White Horse** at Romsey in Hampshire was built at this period on the site of the abbey guesthouse and the remains of the old gallery, now enclosed, may still be seen.

By the beginning of the seventeenth century the English inn was already well established. A great European traveller of this period, Fynes Moryson, tells us in his *Itinerary* (1617) that 'the world affords no such inns as England hath either for pleasure or cheap entertainment'. Nevertheless, there were many places that were still ill-served. Moreoever, the Civil War put an end to inn building. At the end of the seventeenth century Celia Fiennes, the noted traveller and writer, often had difficulty in finding a good lodging. Of a journey to Beverley she wrote:

> . . . here we could get no accommodation at a Publick House, it being a sad poor thatched place and only two or three sorry Ale-houses, no lodgings but at the Hall House as it was called . . . being the Lord of the Mannours house.

In the middle of the seventeenth century, shopkeepers and innkeepers often had difficulties over money because of the serious shortage of small change. Between 1648 and 1673 many of them issued tokens for use locally. John Evelyn, the diarist, refers to 'the tokens which every tavern and tippling house presumed to stamp and utter for immediate exchange'. He goes on to say that these were only passable in the immediate neighbourhood, which seldom reached further than a street or two.

The urgent need for more provision for travellers came with the improvement of the roads which followed the first Turnpike Act in 1663 though the system did not spread rapidly until after 1710. The eighteenth century was a great period for inn building and particularly for the improvement and enlargement of existing inns. By 1770 the roads were very greatly improved and most of them were subject to tolls. They were crowded with traffic—coaches, post-chaises and horses-riders. The first mail coach completed the journey from London to Bristol in 1784. Horses could only be used over a limited distance and the inns had extensive stabling for horses which had to be changed at each 'stage' of the journey. Private carriages or post-chaises also changed their horses at the posting houses. At this period many a Tudor inn was given a more pretentious Georgian frontage and often an assembly room. Such inns became important social centres, attracting the nobility and gentry, and innkeepers became people of importance, often members of the local council or corporation. Council meetings were often held at the inn and the refreshments taken became a charge on the rates. Magistrates courts also used the inns and the assembly rooms became centres where banquets, dances, concerts and public meetings were held. **The Ship** at Brighton, **The Dolphin** at Southampton, and **The Lion** at Shrewsbury are examples of inns which played an important part in the social life of the day.

Early in the nineteenth century when the works of Thomas

Telford and John McAdam had produced still better road surfaces, traffic increased in volume and pace. Between 1803 and 1823 over 1,000 miles of good roads with new bridges were built and by 1835 most main roads had been macadamised. This was the golden age of coaching and the most prosperous period for the keepers of roadside inns. But it was not to last for long.

In the 1830s competition from newly built railways began to hit the coaching trade and, of course, the coaching inns. By 1845 most long distance passenger traffic had been captured by through train services and many of these inns were sold. Some became local public houses; others private residences. Standards in general began to fall and in 1869 the Wine and Beerhouse Act gave local justices control over premises where liquor could be consumed, a power they retain to this day. Road traffic was mainly local, connecting towns and villages with the nearest railway station. By 1895 the turnpike system was dead.

Already, however, new mechanical methods of road transport had begun the great revival of the English inn. The first journey from London to Brighton by bicycle had been made on a 'boneshaker' in 1869. In 1886 the Cyclists' Touring Club and the National Cyclists' Union formed the Road Improvement Association to press for better roads. Country inns began to cater for the touring cyclists, providing accommodation and meals. By 1937 The Cyclists' Touring Club had 4,000 inns on their books carrying the club sign and providing bed and breakfast. This sign may still be seen on some inns—**The Bell** at Bethersden in Kent, for example. **The Anchor Inn** at Ripley in Surrey became a mecca for cyclists and later for motorcyclists who rode down from London and back in the day.

After World War I, with the rapidly increasing popularity of the motor car, the revival of the English inn became certain. Some of the old coaching inns were rescued and restored, new inns were built and many sleazy public houses began to gain an aura of respectability. In the 1930s many roadhouses were built with swimming pools, dance halls and restaurants to attract young people from the nearest town though very few of these roadhouses have survived as such.

After World War II the most significant development was the growth of the motel or 'post house'. Although the number of licensed houses dropped by nearly one third between 1900 and 1970, more people used them and there was less drunkenness. At the same time the number of hotel and restaurant licences increased and the number of private clubs trebled.

Increasing trade made it possible for the brewing companies and hotel chains which now own most of the old inns to make major 'improvements'. The more enlightened managed to retain the interesting architectural features of the old buildings or to restore them. Many of the old class-conscious Victorian bars were torn out and replaced by comfortable lounges. **The Ship** at Herne Bay is a striking example of an internal change planned to meet new demands largely created by women anxious to join their menfolk in a friendly atmosphere, preferably where food is also available.

Change will continue. Yet the successful marriage of old and new demands careful and imaginative planning combined with a high order of workmanship. **The Hatchet Inn** at Bristol and the **Green Dragon Inn** in Lincoln show what can be done in urban surroundings. **The Swan** at Lavenham is a remarkable blend of restoration and rebuilding in a country town. One can only hope that the inevitable changes involved in urban and rural 'renewal' will not impair the character or destroy the atmosphere of the historic English inns.

Page 17: *(above)* The Star, Alfriston ; *(below)* The Royal Albion Hotel, Broadstairs

Page 18: *(above)* Ceiling boss in The Lion, Buckden ; *(below)* The Queen's Hotel, Cheltenham

Historic English Inns

ALFRISTON, Sussex

The Star is one of the finest surviving examples of an old English hostelry. Alfriston (Alwriceston in Domesday Book) lies in a gap in the South Downs through which the River Cuckmere flows to Cuckmere Haven on the Channel coast, a distance of some 4 miles from the village. The valley has been used by invaders seeking a place to settle, by pilgrims resting on their way to the shrine of St Richard at Chichester, and by smugglers bringing their illicit wares inland. The Star was founded in the thirteenth century, probably as The Star of Bethlehem, and parts of the present building date from about 1450. It was built and owned by the abbey of Battle, and was a hospice for pilgrims on their way to the abbey or to Chichester. The timbered frontage which has an overhanging upper storey with three oriel windows is late fifteenth century (see p 17). The roof is of heavy slabs of Horsham stone. Until 1902 the front was covered in plaster; perhaps that is why the carved timbers are so well preserved. These show a figure in robes holding a globe in his right hand, his left hand on his breast and a stag couchant at his feet—said to be St Julian, the friend of travellers. The arms of the De Echyngham family are carved on a pillar; as wealthy local landowners they had almost certainly contributed to abbey funds. Above the doorway and below the centre window are two snakes, their tails entwined, supporting a niche. There is also a grotesque group with St Michael fighting an amphisbaena—a dragon or serpent with forked tongue and with a second head on its tail. At the corner of the inn is a figurehead in the form of a red lion, said to have been taken from a

Dutch vessel, possibly one of the De Ruyter's ships wrecked off Birling Gap, east of Cuckmere Haven, after the battle of Sole Bay in 1672.

The interior of The Star has massive moulded beams, chamfered joists and a stone fireplace, the cornice held by angel corbels. A wall-post bears the letters I.H.S. The bar to the right of the entrance was once the inn kitchen and has a fine early fireplace.

In the 1780s race meetings were held on the southern slope of Firle Beacon and the horses were entered at the Star Inn which provided a good 'ordinary' for the racegoers. At this period a club for buying and selling corn met at the inn.[1]

The **Market Cross Inn,** often known as Ye Olde Smugglers Inn, at the northern end of the village, was once a large private house. It is 600 years old, black-beamed and now faced with whitewashed tiles and weatherboarding. Towards the end of the eighteenth century it was the home of Stanton Collins, a noted smuggler—not that he needed to live a life of crime for he had respectable parents and was happily married. Nevertheless smuggling had a fascination for him and he led the Alfriston Gang, bringing contraband into Cuckmere Haven and stealing pigs and sheep from downland farms, a crime for which he was eventually hanged.

ALRESFORD, Hampshire

The Swan in West Street is notable for its connection with the famous case of the Tichborne Claimant. The Tichborne estate lies 2 miles south-west of Alresford and in early Victorian times its business was conducted by local solicitors whose chief clerk was Edward Rous. In the 1860s Rous became landlord of the Swan. On 29 December 1866, a visitor registered in the name of Taylor and struck up a friendship with the landlord. Next day they drove together to Tichborne and Taylor talked much about the Tichborne family and local affairs. So much so that Rous began to think that Taylor must be none other than Roger Charles Tichborne, the heir to the Tichborne estate, despite the fact that it had been assumed that Roger had been lost at sea some years previously. Shortly afterwards Taylor was hailed by Lady Tichborne as her long lost son and he actually became claimant to the estate.

In 1868 Lady Tichborne died. There were still some doubts in certain quarters about Taylor's identity and a certain Detective Wicher visited Alresford and convinced Rous that the claimant was in fact Arthur Orton and no relation to the Tichbornes. On 1 February 1869 a meeting was held at the Swan at which the claimant successfully defended himself; Rous who had deserted him became so unpopular that he was forced to sell the hotel and leave the town.

Later, the claimant was arrested, imprisoned for over fifty days and then released on bail. When he expressed his intention of visiting Alresford the new owner of the Swan sent a decorated waggonette to fetch him and the claimant received a great reception in the town from tenants of the estate who regarded him as their rightful landlord. Bands played and there were celebrations which lasted well into the evening, and he was given a dinner at the Swan. Eventually, in 1873, the claimant was forced to face a criminal trial and in 1874 was sentenced to fourteen years penal servitude as an imposter.[2]

AMESBURY, Wiltshire

The George on the A303 has a long history. It started as a pilgrim's hospice attached to Amesbury Abbey. In the reign of Henry VIII it became crown property and in 1541 took the name of The George and Dragon. General Fairfax used the inn in 1645 as a headquarters after he had succeeded Essex as supreme commander of the Parliamentary forces.

In the eighteenth century, as road conditions improved, the inn was remodelled and became an important halfway house for the Quicksilver Mail between London and Exeter. Nevertheless, much of the earlier structure remains.

Some Dickens enthusiasts believe the George to be the Blue Dragon village alehouse of *Martin Chuzzlewit* (1843-4) kept by Mrs Lupin. Others, assert that this alehouse was The Green Dragon at Alderbury, 3 miles south-east of Salisbury. It seems more likely, however, that Dickens presented a composite picture based on more than one of the Wiltshire inns he knew.

ANDOVER, Hampshire

The Angel in Upper High Street, originally the College Inn, is the oldest inn in Andover, dating from the twelfth century. King John stayed in the inn when he gave the borough its charter in 1201, and other royal visitors are said to have included Edward I and Edward II.

In 1435 the College Inn was destroyed by fire and was rebuilt in 1444-5 by the owners, Winchester College, to a plan prepared by the master carpenter of Eton College. This was a galleried inn and traces of the old gallery may still be seen though it is now enclosed. The timber structure of the rest of the building is largely intact and the interior shows heavy beams supported by posts rising from a flagged floor. The timbers of the High Street frontage, however, are hidden by a later brick-built external wall.

The rebuilt inn eventually became The Angel. Its first royal visitor was Henry VII. In 1501 Catherine of Aragon stayed at the Angel when travelling from Plymouth to London. Richard Pope, grandfather of Alexander Pope, held the lease from 1582-1633. In 1622 he was the Bailiff of Andover.[3] When his will was proved in 1633 it listed twenty-six rooms in the Angel besides larders, cellars, barns etc, each with its distinguishing name: '. . . the half moone, the crosskeys, the crowne, the lyon, the boare, the starr, the fawlcon, the rose, the squirrel, the angell, the unicorn . . .'

When James II was retreating from William of Orange in 1688 he took a meal at the inn with Prince George and the Duke of Ormonde who thereafter left the king to his fate.

The Angel was involved in the agricultural riots of 1830-1 when a mob invaded the town and Bethell Coxe, a local magistrate, addressed them from a window but failed to pacify them. Next day the troops had to be called in.[4]

In the nineteenth century part of the inn was sold and more recently, in the 1960s, its very existence was threatened. Happily it escaped being engulfed by 'development' and now stands on the edge of a modern shopping precinct.

The George, an inn since 1576, is approached through an archway on the south side of the High Street. It is mainly remembered for a prosperous landlord called Sutton who wore a 'round-skirted sleeved fustian waistcoat, with a dirty white apron tied round his middle'. In 1826, when William Cobbett was making a speech about the Corn Laws in the Market Room of the George, the interest was so great that members of the audience failed to refill their tankards. Sutton then tried to make things difficult for the speaker. This angered Cobbett and also the audience, and Sutton narrowly escaped being thrown out of his own house.

The Star and Garter at the southern end of the High Street dates back to 1582, or possibly earlier, when it was known as The White Hart. The present building dates from 1827. It has three storeys with large bow windows on the first and second floors. A central portico with fluted Ionic pillars supports a railed balcony.

Charles I stayed at the inn in 1644 after a successful clash with Cromwell's troops and before proceeding to Whitchurch and Newbury. George III stayed at the inn on a number of occasions when travelling to Weymouth. The first was in 1778 when the Company of Haberdashers presented him with a loyal address. (This was the year when the inn became the Star and Garter.) George III also paid a visit with Queen Charlotte in 1801. A year previously Lord Nelson had stayed at the inn with Lady Hamilton and her mother.

The White Hart in Bridge Street dates from 1671 when it was known as the Lower Starre. It became the White Hart soon after its near neighbour—the Star and Garter—changed its name in 1788.

Andover was a very important centre for coach traffic in the eighteenth and early nineteenth centuries and at this period the White Hart was a large coaching inn with stabling for seventy-five horses. After the decline in coach traffic there was a break in its history as an inn. In 1849 it was sold and became the workshop for a coachbuilder, Thomas Pontin, who lived on the premises. It reopened as an inn in 1852.

ASHBOURNE, Derbyshire

The Green Man or, to give it its full name **The Green Man and**

Black's Head Royal, is a three-storey brick building, mainly Georgian, though it was a prosperous inn at the beginning of the eighteenth century. There is a large yard entrance from which a flight of steps leads to the dining room. During the eighteenth century the magistrates of the Hundred of Low Peat met at the inn. At this time it was a centre for the sport of cockfighting.

Dr Johnson and James Boswell stayed at the Green Man several times and Boswell refers to it as 'very good' and the mistress as a 'mighty civil gentlewoman'.[5]

The inn has a fine gallows sign spanning the street. On it rests the effigy of the 'Black's Head' and below swings a painted sign showing a forester wearing a green coat, standing with dog and gun. The full name of the hotel is carried on the beam; it derives from the amalgamation of two inns which were once face to face. The 'Royal' was added after a visit by Queen Victoria.

AYLESBURY, Bucks

The King's Head at the north-west corner of the Market Square has no road frontage. It is approached through a cobbled way between two shops. The timber-framed building dates from about 1450 and almost certainly started as a hospice attached to the Greyfriars' monastery which was founded by Sir James Botelier in 1386. The earliest reference to the building in 1455 is of 'three messuages called KYNGESHEDE'—a shop, a cellar beneath it, and a cottage.

Inside the inn is a fine hall in which the ceiling is supported by massive oak posts. The large mullioned contemporary wooden window contains twenty lights, some with old heraldic stained glass. The first four shields have been damaged and are set back to front. The first shows the arms of England and France (quarterly) for Henry VI, and the fourth the arms of Anjou (quarterly for six) for Queen Margaret. (The latter are the same, but for the omission of a green border, as those of Queen's College, Cambridge, of which Margaret of Anjou was one of the royal founders.) The arms of their son who was killed at the Battle of Tewkesbury are also to be seen.

In the upper lights are the remains of a series of angels holding shields, the winged lion of St Mark with a scroll inscribed 'Marcus', original quarries with flower designs, the covered cup of the Boteliers (Butlers), and the chained swan of the de Bohuns. The Butlers, Earls of Ormonde, were lords of the manor of Aylesbury in the fourteenth and fifteenth centuries. The de Bohun chained swan has long been linked with the arms of Buckinghamshire. The hall contains many fine carved beams and the old wattle and daub wall construction is exposed in one place between the timber uprights.

The King's Head became an inn in the reign of Henry VIII who is said to have stayed here during his courtship of Anne Boleyn whose father was Lord of the Manor of Aylesbury.

During the Civil War, Aylesbury was a Parliamentary stronghold and the scene of one of the early engagements in 1643. It was in Aylesbury that Cromwell received the thanks of Parliament at the end of the Civil War in 1651. It is not surprising therefore, to find that there is a bedroom in the King's Head where Cromwell slept, with a listening hole which enables the occupant to hear conversation in the hall below. In 1657 the innkeeper, William Dawney, issued a trade token, an impression of which is exhibited in a showcase.

In the eighteenth and nineteenth centuries the King's Head became a coaching inn. The courtyard is still cobbled and the old wooden entrance gates which protected the inn at night are still in place.

Various manuscripts relating to the inn, which was given to the National Trust by the widow and family of the Hon Charles Rothschild in 1925, are preserved in the Birmingham Public Library. They include an inventory of the inn furniture made c1650.

BARNARD CASTLE, Durham

The King's Head, in the Market Place, was used by Charles Dickens and Hablot Browne, his illustrator, when they arrived at Barnard Castle after travelling by post chaise from the Morritt Arms at Greta Bridge on 2 February 1838. Dickens was collecting material for *Nicholas Nickleby* (1838-9). Early in the nineteenth century this part of the country was noted for its 'cheap' boarding schools and Dickens, anxious to see one, chose Bowes Academy, a school presided over by a master called Wiliam Shaw. To avoid suspicion he took an assumed name and presented a formal letter from a fictitious London solicitor explaining that he was acting for the widowed mother of a small boy who was considering sending the lad to a boarding school. Dickens saw the school and was horrified. It is said that a local farmer who had heard of the proposal to send a London boy to the school arranged to meet Dickens at the Unicorn Inn at Bowes to urge him to persuade the mother not to send him to such a wretched place 'while there's a harse to hoold in a' Lunnon, or a goother to be asleep in'.

Barnard Castle provided Dickens with the title for another publication. Looking across the road from the coffee room of The Kings' Head, he saw a shop, with the sign 'Humphreys, Clockmaker' above the doorway. *Master Humphrey's Clock* became the title for a series of miscellaneous stories he projected, though the original idea was soon abandoned in favour of two full-length novels—*The Old Curiosity Shop* and *Barnaby Rudge*—which were issued in parts under this overall title in 1840 and 1841.

BATH, Somerset

The Francis Hotel in Queen Square consists of six Georgian houses (Nos 6-11), four of which were damaged in the 'Baedeker raid' on Bath in April 1942 and were later carefully rebuilt in the same style. The square was designed by John Wood the Elder and built by Samuel Emes between 1729 and 1736. It was probably Wood's masterpiece.

Queen Square, named after George II's Queen Caroline, was the first of Bath's eighteenth-century squares, a fashionable centre of private houses many of which later became lodging houses. Several of them have interesting associations. It is almost certain that John Wood the Elder lived in No 9 and it is said that he died in Queen Square. In 1799 Jane Austen lodged at No 13 with a Mrs Bromley who kept lodgings at Nos 12 and 13 adjoining the Francis Hotel on the west side.

In July 1814, Harriet Westbrook, Shelley's wife, came to live at No 6 after her husband had left her and eloped to the Continent with Mary Godwin. This house is now part of the hotel.

BATTLE, Sussex

The Pilgrim's Rest was a hospice attached to Battle Abbey which was built soon after the Norman Conquest. The hospice is known to have existed early in the fourteenth century and was probably used by poor travellers on their way to Hastings to cross the Channel.[6] Today it is a licensed restaurant.

The building consists of a hall of two bays with a wing of two storeys on each side. The timber construction shows clearly: the hall timbers are set on a stone footing, and there are cross-beams and curved struts. A fine octagonal king-post with moulded capital and base rises from a main truss to the centre of the roof. These beams were revealed during restoration.

The George, built in the eighteenth century on the site of an earlier inn, was designed to serve the increasing traffic through the town. In 1712 it was described as 'George with the gardens': these were hop gardens cultivated by the landlord who brewed his own beer. The inn was later recognised as the main meeting place for local people. Public meetings were held in the inn from 1771; the magistrates' court met there from 1782 and during the Napoleonic Wars it became the military headquarters for the higher officers of the local command. The Royal Mail coaches stopped at the George on alternate days since the trade was shared with **The Star** (previously the Eight Bells), a Georgian inn rebuilt in 1800 which lies close to the abbey. The George, however, was the chief inn. William Cobbett stayed there on 4 January 1822:

> I had no time to see the town, having entered the Inn on Wednesday in the dusk of the evening, having been engaged all day yesterday at the Inn, and having come out of it only to get into the coach this morning. I have not time even to see the Abbey.

The coach traffic declined rapidly after 1852 when the railway came to Battle.

BEDFORD

The Swan, on the bank of the River Ouse, stands on the site of earlier inns. There was an inn there when Henry VII seized the crown of England after the battle of Bosworth in 1485 and a later coaching inn had records dating back to 1507. The present stone-faced building was designed by Henry Holland for the Duke of Bedford c1792-4. It has four storeys, the upper one with a pediment which spans the façade, and a bracket cornice surrounds the building. The wide porch on four Ionic columns supports a balcony. On the river side there are two semicircular bow windows on the first floor. The interior has a fine old staircase with twisted balusters dating from 1688. This was brought from Houghton House and installed in the Swan Hotel when it was built.

BEENHAM, Berkshire

The Three Kings, or **Jack's Booth,** is a public house on the southern side of the A4 just over 2 miles west of Theale and well over a mile from the village of Beenham which lies in the country to the west. It is an eighteenth-century tiled house of two storeys with shuttered windows on the ground floor and a later enclosed brick porch. On the rounded corner there are two names—The Three Kings (representing the kings who came to pay homage to the infant Jesus), and Jack's Booth, a reminder that a forgotten prizefighter once had a booth behind the inn.

The main interest, however, is in the fact that it was frequented by the Reverend Thomas Stackhouse, MA, a scholarly man who became vicar of Beenham Vallence in 1737. He wrote many books, but could not keep away from the bottle and would sit at a table in the bar of the inn surrounded by books and papers, constantly calling for more beer. His most notable work was the *History of the Holy Bible from the beginning of the World to the Establishment of Christianity,* a book with horrific scenes which frightened Charles Lamb in his childhood.

Stackhouse was dirty and unkempt and often the worse for liquor even in the pulpit where he preached sermons full of maudlin appeals to the Almighty for forgiveness. One day he was dragged from the inn, half drunk, to face the bishop whose intended visit he had forgotten. 'Who is this shabby old man?' asked the bishop. 'I am the vicar of Beenham Vallence' shouted Stackhouse 'who wrote the History of the Bible which is more than your Lordship could do.' This was the end of his incumbency. Nevertheless, he lived on, still drinking heavily, but making a great deal of money from his writings. He died at the age of seventy-five and was buried in the churchyard at Beenham.

BEVERLEY, Yorkshire (East Riding)

The Beverley Arms in North Bar Within was known in 1666 as the Blue Bell Inn or Blew Bell Inn. It was used in that year by Sir William Dugdale, Garter King of Arms, as a place where he could meet local people who wished to register their coats of arms and pedigrees with the Herald's College. Little remains of the original inn; it was rebuilt c1700 and again early in the 1790s when the name was changed to the Beverley Arms. It is a three-storey brick building with a Tuscan porch surmounted by a balcony. In the eighteenth century the inn was an important centre with stabling for over a hundred horses, from which coaches left for Scarborough, Hull and York. It was in the yard of the old Blue Bell that Dick Turpin was seen on a stolen black gelding in 1738. In 1737, after shooting Tom King in London, Turpin had fled to the East Riding of Yorkshire and set up as a horse dealer under the name of Palmer. In 1738 he was arrested on suspicion and the magistrates were prepared to dismiss the case but he was unable to find sureties for his good behaviour. Further enquiries revealed his identity and he was convicted of horse stealing. The theft of the black gelding was one of the charges. He was hanged in York on 10 April 1739.

The Beverley Arms continued as an important inn into the nineteenth century. Some idea of its character in late Victorian days is given by two paintings of its large stone-flagged kitchen by F. W. Elwell, RA, a local artist who lived at Bar House near the inn. One hangs in the Tate Gallery, the other in the Walker Art Gallery, Liverpool. The old kitchen has now been turned into a buttery.

BINFIELD, Berkshire

The Stag and Hounds which dates from the fourteenth century was probably at one time a hunting lodge in the centre of Windsor Forest when the forest covered almost the whole of East Berkshire. An old hollow elm, known as the 'centre elm', which has hidden many a miscreant, still stands on the old village green in front of the inn. In Elizabethan times the forest rangers and their families used the green for carnivals and Queen Elizabeth is said to have watched pole dancing from the inn windows.

In Georgian times the Stag and Hounds became a coaching house and during the Regency a new wing was built which now abuts on the B3034. William Cobbett spoke highly of the inn when on a journey from Kensington to Wokingham in 1822.

The interior of the central and oldest part of the Stag and Hounds is full of heavy oak beams, mainly original. In one door is an inset of decorated stained glass which was rescued from Westminster Chapel during the bombing of World War II.

BOLVENTOR, Cornwall

Jamaica Inn at Bolventor in the centre of Bodmin Moor, a grey building of local stone and slate, was in existence in the eighteenth century and no doubt served travellers on the indifferent road to west Cornwall. It is known to have been called Jamaica Inn in the 1780s, possibly because of a traffic in rum. The name of the tiny settlement of Bolventor which grew up round the inn appears to have referred to the 'bold venture' in setting up such an establishment in so remote a place. The inn served as a posting house for well over a hundred years but in 1893 for a short period became Bolventor Temperance Hotel before resuming its earlier functions. Bolventor was the setting for Daphne du Maurier's novel *Jamaica Inn* (1936).

BOX HILL, Surrey

The Burford Bridge Hotel lies on the A24 in the wooded gap in the North Downs between Leatherhead and Dorking. North to south travellers from the London area must cross the River Mole at this point and in 1755 Burford Bridge was built to take the expanding coach traffic bound for Brighton via Dorking. As a result, a seventeenth-century house close to the bridge was made into an inn—The Fox and Hounds. In the nineteenth century this was enlarged and largely rebuilt to become the Burford Bridge Hotel. Its large garden with a fine box walk rises steeply to Box Hill (600ft), now National Trust property.

Many famous people have used the inn over the years. Lord Nelson stayed here with Emma Hamilton on several occasions including short periods during the summers of 1801 and 1802 but not, as is so often stated, on the night before he sailed for Trafalgar.

Keats completed *Endymion* at the inn for on the last page of the draft he wrote: 'Burford Bridge, Nov. 28 1817'. This was the culmination of seven months of concentrated work and he then stayed on at the inn for a while to rest.

Robert Louis Stevenson wrote parts of his *New Arabian Nights* (1882) at the Burford Bridge while on a visit in 1878 when he formed a friendship with George Meredith who lived at Flint Cottage nearby, a friendship renewed during a second visit in 1882.

Many other writers used the inn—Richard Brinsley Sheridan, Robert Southey, William Wordsworth and William Hazlitt who delighted to read under the shade of the apple tree in the garden. Queen Victoria also stayed in the hotel before her accession.

In 1935 a seventeenth-century tithe barn was removed from Abinger Manor and re-erected under the direction of Mr Harry Redfern as an addition to the Burford Bridge Hotel, though the aisles, gallery and ingle nook are additions.[7]

BRIDGWATER, Somerset

The Royal Clarence in Cornhill, opposite the Market Hall, was built in the Regency style on the site of two earlier inns, the Angel and the Crown. It was opened in 1825 as 'The Royal

Hotel'[8] and became The Royal Clarence Hotel after a visit by the Duchess of Clarence, afterwards Queen Adelaide, on 6 August 1828. The hotel, probably designed by Benjamin Baker, is a three-storey stuccoed building with a central portico supporting a balcony on four Ionic pillars. The arms of Bridgwater above the portico were brought from the old iron bridge over the River Parrett when it was demolished in 1883. Inside there is a fine assembly room with a musician's gallery. There is a lettered sign on the façade of the hotel between the first and second floors.

The Royal Clarence was for some time an important posting house used by the Royal Mail (Bristol and Barnstaple) and the Old Bath Coach (Bath and Exeter).

BRIDPORT, Dorset

The Bull, or **Knight's Bull,** is on the A35 trunk road between Bournemouth and Exeter. It dates from the sixteenth century and became a noted coaching inn, a stopping place for the 'Royal Mail' from London to Exeter and Falmouth, the 'Celerity' from London to Exeter via Salisbury and Dorchester, the 'Eclipse' from London to Falmouth, and the 'Regulator' from London to Exeter. Post-chaises were also available. Later, when the railway reached Bridport, the Bull ran its own coach between Bridport Station and Lyme Regis. In the grill room a mural shows Monmouth and his supporters landing in Dorset.

The Greyhound Hotel, further west on the same side of the A35, is an eighteenth-century inn which was noted as a farmers' meeting place. A notice inside the yard entrance refers to the inn thus:

> The place fixed for the delivery of the corn returns within this town is the Greyhound Hotel where an officer of customs and excise will attend as Inspector of Corn returns, to receive corn returns on the day on which such returns are required by law to be made.

Opposite the Greyhound is a chemists shop which was once the **Old George** where Charles II came on 23 September 1651.

BRIGHTON, Sussex

The Old Ship in King's Road faces the sea roughly midway between Brighton's two piers. The original inn on this site was owned c1670 by Captain Nicholas Tettersell who had carried Charles II across the English Channel to Fecamp in Normandy in a coal brig in 1651. He received payment for his services and in 1663, when Charles II had been restored to the throne, was granted a pension of £100 a year. He is said to have had an inn in 'The Lanes' and to have moved to The Old Ship Tavern in a more fashionable part of Brighthelmstone, as Brighton was then called.[9]

The Ship was rebuilt in 1755 and became the terminus for the London coaches and an important social centre in the town. Fanny Burney was invited to dine there in 1779 with Mr and Mrs Thrale in the officers' mess of the Sussex Militia. In 1789 a magnificent ball was held on the occasion of the birthday of the Prince of Wales. The prince, who was celebrating at the Pavilion, put in an appearance and joined in some of the dances. *The New Brighton Guide* of 1796 refers to a weekly ball held on Thursdays and to the card assemblies on Wednesdays and Fridays. Mrs Fitzherbert was patroness of the balls at the Old Ship Hotel for a number of years but gave it up in 1830 and wrote that she had some difficulty in finding ladies to take her place.

Charles Dickens stayed at the Old Ship in 1841 when he was working on *Barnaby Rudge* (1840-1) and William Makepeace Thackeray worked in the hotel on the early parts of *Vanity Fair* (1847-8).

BRISTOL

The Grand Spa in Clifton, overlooking the Avon Gorge, was built in 1893 when the magazine and newspaper proprietor, George Newnes, planned the hydraulic cliff railway from Hotwells Road to Sion Hill, now closed. Newnes was fascinated by cliff railways—he built the one from Lynton to Lynmouth—and he was given permission to construct the Clifton one on condition that he revived the old Clifton spa by building a pump room at the end of Prince's Buildings. From the very beginning the enterprise seemed doomed to failure and the building finally became an ordinary hotel. The ornate building which once housed the spring-water and mineral baths can still be seen with the initials G.N. woven in the masonry.

The Hatchet in Frogmore Street is probably the oldest building in the city, though it has undergone many changes and much restoration. The sixteenth-century timbers were once covered with lath and plaster; the timbers of the façade have now been exposed and restored. Most of the old windows were replaced by sash windows in the eighteenth century. Early features inside include part of a staircase and a plaster ceiling on the first floor.

At one time the Hatchet was on the main road to Clifton (before Park Street existed) and for a period in the nineteenth century it was frequented by prizefighters including Thomas Cribb, Tom Sayers and Jem Mace.

Urban development in the 1960s threatened its existence but it survived and is now close to a main road once more. It was restored so well that in 1969 it won a Civic Trust award for 'a successful piece of urban surgery dealing imaginatively with the situation created by a new road on the edge of an historic area'.

The Llandoger Trow is in seventeenth-century King Street in the centre of the city. Originally it consisted of five gabled private houses. Two of these were badly damaged in the air raids of 1940 and were pulled down. The frontage of the inn is half-timbered and there is much original timbering and plasterwork inside. The houses were built in 1664 but they were not made into an inn until the end of the eighteenth century, possibly even later. The name was that of a ship in which Captain Hawkins traded from the nearby quay.

Robert Louis Stevenson is said to have chosen the Llandoger Trow as the setting for the beginning of *Treasure Island* (1883). Notable visitors to the inn were actors and actresses who played at the Theatre Royal on the opposite side of the street, among them Sir Henry Irving, Wilson Barrett, Sir Herbert Beerbohm Tree and Kate Terry.

The Rummer is in All Saint's Lane which leads from Corn Street to the Markets. There was an inn on this site called The

Page 35: *(right)* Carved panels on the façade of The Red Lion, Colchester; *(below)* The Bear, Devizes

Page 36: *(above)* The Luttrell Arms, Dunster; *(left)* The George and Pilgrims, Glastonbury

Greene Lattis in 1241. Then came The Abyndon, named after the owner of the premises, Henry Abyndon, who was a noted musician. Later it became The Jonas and by the middle of the sixteenth century it had taken the name The New Star. It became an important coaching establishment which had an entrance from the High Street. In the eighteenth century, when it had become The Rummer Tavern, the front of the inn was rebuilt and a new approach made. This was part of the scheme designed by John Wood The Elder in 1743 when he was engaged as architect for the building of Bristol Corn Exchange. Many famous people have used The Rummer including Queen Elizabeth, Charles I, Charles II, William III and Oliver Cromwell.

The Shakespeare in Victoria Street is a timber-framed building dating from 1636 though there is no record of the inn in what was then Temple Street in the first Bristol directory of 1775. Apart from the insertion of sash windows, the inn remains much as it was in the seventeenth century with two storeys with bays and a single large overhanging gable.

BROADSTAIRS, Kent

The Royal Albion Hotel in Albion Street overlooks the harbour. It was partly built before 1816 and was completed before 1820 when it was known as Ballard's. The highest part has four storeys with a balcony at first-floor level. A dining room and lounge verandah extend on the seaward side from ground-floor level. The hotel now incorporates several old houses, one of them a lodging house in which Charles Dickens stayed in 1839 and wrote the latter part of *Nicholas Nickleby*.

Dickens was greatly attracted to Broadstairs. In a letter from Italy he reveals his nostalgia:

> I have never seen it so clear, for any long time of the day together, as on a bright lark-singing day at Broadstairs.

In a letter which hangs in the hotel he writes:

> A good sea, fresh breezes, fine sand and pleasant walks, with all manner of fishing boats, lighthouses, piers, bathing

machines are its only attractions; but it is one of the freshest and freest places in the world.

Dickens stayed in the Albion for periods in 1845, in 1849 when he wrote part of *David Copperfield*, and again in 1859 despite the fact that he had already described the town as having become 'far too noisy'.

BROADWAY, Worcestershire

The Lygon Arms on the northern side of Broadway's main street dates from 1530 when it was known as The Whyte Harte. Since then there have been changes and additions but this building of warm, brown stone with its four great gables, mullioned windows and towering chimneys remains a superb example of Cotswold architecture. The Jacobean doorway was added by John and Ursula Treavis in 1620. Treavis was landlord of The Whyte Harte from 1604 to 1641 and his name, with that of his wife, appears on the carved woodwork. He was also responsible for interior features including the stone fireplace and the plasterwork in the room which Cromwell is said to have used in 1651 before the battle of Worcester. There is also a panelled room which was almost certainly used by Charles I and his supporters.

In the eighteenth century the inn flourished as a coaching house. In 1767 the landlord was Giles Attwood and a record of 1787 comments on the fatness of its dogs. It was still doing well when, between 1815 and 1820, it came into the hands of General Edward Lygon who served under Wellington at Waterloo. His butler took over the inn on the understanding that it should bear the general's name and from that time it has been known as The Lygon Arms. (The General was the son of the first Earl Beauchamp of Madresfield Court, Malvern.) As the years went by and horsedrawn traffic declined with the coming of the railways, the inn also declined. The revival did not come until 1904 when, by great good fortune, it was acquired by Sidney Bolton Russell, a connoisseur who not only restored the fabric but brought in fine period furniture appropriate to the setting.

BUCKDEN, Huntingdonshire

The Lion at the junction of Church Street and the old Great North Road (now bypassed) has been known at various times as The Lion and Lamb, The Lamb and Flag, and simply as The Lamb. It adopted the Lion as its sign in the 1860s to commemorate its past association with the See of Lincoln for it started as a guest house for the palace of Bishops of Lincoln. It was built c1490 and its religious origin is reflected in the fifteenth-century ceiling of moulded oak beams in what was originally the hall of the medieval building. At the junction of the beams, in the middle of the ceiling, is a large central boss carved with the sacred symbol of the lamb and the words *Ecce Agnus Dei* (Behold the Lamb of God) (see p 18). Other survivals of the original building are to be seen but most of it disappeared in the eighteenth century when changes were made to convert the inn into a posting house. The front of the west side was raised, the northern wing extended, and the south wing rebuilt. Externally no ancient features are now to be seen. The façade carries the double name 'The Old Lion and Lamb' and 'The Lion'.

BUCKLER'S HARD, Hampshire

The Master Builder's House is the last house on the left of two rows of red-brick Georgian houses which run down to the 'hard' on the Beaulieu River, where many battleships and merchantmen were built in the eighteenth century.[10] The most famous British shipbuilder of the period was Henry Adams who lived in the Master Builder's House. Between 1749 and his death in 1805 he was responsible for over forty ships, among them the *Agamemnon* with sixty-four guns which was launched in 1781 and captained by Horatio, Lord Nelson in 1783. Banquets to celebrate the launchings were held in the Master Builder's House which was converted into a hotel by John, 2nd Lord Montagu of Beaulieu in 1926.

BURY ST EDMUNDS, Suffolk

The Angel, on the old fairground slope known as Angel Hill, was built as a hospice for the Abbey of Edmundsbury in 1452.

It still has medieval cellars with arched vaulting which some say were a charnel house to which priests would retire to sing masses for the souls of those whose remains rested in adjoining vaults. Angel Hill is said to be honeycombed with cellars and secret passages.

The inn expanded in the seventeenth century when Bury St Edmunds became a flourishing woollen centre, and again when the coach route from London to Norwich became important. The present Georgian building dates from 1779. It has four storeys and steps lead to the entrance through a pillared portico surmounted by a balcony.

Dickens immortalised The Angel in his novels. The inn figures largely in *Pickwick Papers* (1836-7).

> The coach rattled through the well-paved streets of a handsome little town of thriving and cleanly appearance and stopped before a large inn in a wide open street, nearly facing the old Abbey. 'And this', said Mr. Pickwick looking up, 'is the Angel. We alight here.'

Later Mr. Pickwick was confined to his room in the inn with rheumatism and here he received the news from Dodson and Fogg that Mrs Bardell intended to bring an action against him for breach of promise. It was in the Angel that Mr Pickwick and Sam Weller were so badly misled by Job Trotter.

Dickens knew the Angel well. He stayed at the inn when he was reporting the electoral campaign of 1835 and again when he gave readings in the town in 1859 and 1861. From the inn he wrote, 'Last night I read Copperfield at Bury St Edmunds to a very fine audience. I don't think a word—not to say an idea—was lost.'

In 1963 the Angel incorporated the adjacent St Edmunds Hotel.

CALNE, Wiltshire

Lansdowne Arms in the Strand is close to the Town Hall and occupies most of one side of the old Market Square. It was founded in the sixteenth century as The Catherine Wheel and is mentioned in the borough records of 1582. The old inn was enlarged in the reign of George II when the coaching route to Bath via Calne was becoming more popular at the expense of the Devizes route.

The inn has a long frontage with thirteen windows in each of its two storeys and an unbroken parapet which carries a lettered sign. The entrance to the old courtyard now forms the entrance hall. When viewed from the front, the oldest part of the building is to the left. This carries a huge barometer at first floor level, the needle set by a small barometer (by Yeates of Dublin) in the room behind. The façade also carries an old firemark.

The inn was named Lansdowne Arms between 1824 and 1829 and continued as part of the estate of the Lansdowne family of Bowood until 1925.

CAMBRIDGE

The Blue Boar in Trinity Street certainly existed in 1693 when, according to the parish records, the churchwardens of All Saints Church spent two shillings 'for Beer at ye Blue Boar on Ye Queen's Birthday'. The name was probably taken from that of an earlier inn on the opposite side of the street which is known to have existed in 1552.

In the eighteenth century the Blue Boar became an important coaching inn. In 1798, the landlord, John Mound, who was the Bishop of Ely's former butler, advertised coaches departing for London, Sheffield, Birmingham, Ipswich and Norwich. Early in the nineteenth century there was a major reconstruction and later the courtyard was covered in. Part of the ground floor of the four-storey building with shuttered windows, is now occupied by a bank. The decline of the coaching trade is reflected in the following verse by a coachman, Tom Cross, who regularly called at the Blue Boar. It is part of 'The Lament and Anticipation of a Stage Coachman'.

> The smiling chambermaid, she too, forlorn,
> The boots' gruff voice, the waiter's busy zest,
> The ostler's whistle, or the guard's loud horn,
> No more shall call them from their place of rest.

The Eagle, formerly **The Eagle and the Child,** is approached from Bene't Street through an entrance which leads across its yard to the private car park of Corpus Christi College. It dates from the early part of the seventeenth century but the main interest is in the Regency gallery (c1815) supported by iron pillars. It was in the Eagle that John Mortlock, thirteen times mayor of Cambridge between 1784 and his death in 1816, a member of Parliament at the age of twenty-nine, the first man to found a bank in the town and the most influential citizen, established the Rutland Club. Here all the influential townsmen who supported the Duke of Rutland's Whig policies were liberally entertained. The duke represented the university in the House of Commons between 1774 and 1779. In the eighteenth and nineteenth centuries The Eagle was an important coaching inn.

CANTERBURY, Kent

The Falstaff lies outside the Westgate in St Dunstan's Street and was built in 1403 to provide hospitality for the pilgrims who arrived at the city when the gates had been locked after curfew. It was then known as the White Hart. There are a number of Tudor features. The two upper storeys overhang beneath a hipped tiled roof. The lattice windows are probably eighteenth century. Inside are fine moulded beams and some early panelling.

The name was changed to The Falstaff in 1783 and in the nineteenth century a massive wrought iron bracket sign was erected which caused some trouble. In 1863 the Canterbury Pavement Commissioners ordered the owner, a Mrs Crodsdile, to have it removed. Eventually, however, a compromise was reached and she paid one shilling a year to keep the sign, certainly the most impressive in Canterbury today. On the opposite side of St Dunstan's street, at No 71, is a small hotel with three storeys and three gables, called **The House of Agnes.** This house is described by Dickens in *David Copperfield* (1849-50).

Within the city walls there were many inns. Some were destroyed in the air raids of World War II. One of the oldest to survive is no longer an inn but still carries the sign— **The Sun Hotel**. This was at one time the Sun Inn, a three-storey building dating from 1503 with overhanging upper storeys. An earlier inn which existed as early as 1205 near the Christchurch Gateway was used by servants of the monastery. In 1675 it ceased to be an inn and this is probably the date when the licence passed to the Sun. It was well known to Dickens and is the Little Inn of *David Copperfield*. Here it was that Mr Micawber was seen sitting by a window 'waiting for something to turn up'. Today the ground floor has been converted into shops.

CHARLTON, Wiltshire

The Charlton Cat (formerly the Poore's Arms), a public house about 2 miles west of Upavon on the A342, is associated with Stephen Duck, a farm labourer born in the village in 1705. He started work at the age of fourteen and married when he was nineteen but, after bearing him three children, his wife died in 1730. Meanwhile, Duck had been trying to improve his education and had started to write poetry. Some of his poems were read to Queen Caroline at Windsor in 1730 and three years later she made Duck a yeoman of the guard and put him in charge of a library at Richmond Park with a yearly pension. Shortly afterwards Duck married Mrs Sarah Big, housekeeper to Queen Caroline. In 1746 he was ordained and became vicar of Byfleet in Surrey.

Stephen Duck is remembered more for the royal patronage than for the quality of his poems. Jonathan Swift expressed a professional and contemporary view:

> From threshing corn he turns to thresh his brains,
> For which Her Majesty allows him gains,
> Tho' 'tis confessed that those who ever saw
> His poems think them all not worth a straw,
> Thrice happy Duck! Employed in threshing stubble,
> Thy toil is lessened, and thy profits double.

Unhappy in his second marriage and depressed by the reactions to his verse, Duck eventually left London in 1756 and set out for his native village which he failed to reach. He drowned himself in a stream near Reading and was buried in Sonning Churchyard.

One of his poems—'A Journey to Marlborough'—was inscribed to the Lord Palmerston of that day who gave the rent of some land and a cottage at Rushall to provide an annual 'Duck Feast' at the village tavern. This is still held every year in June at The Charlton Cat where there are some Duck relics in the lounge bar, including two editions of his *Poems on Several Occasions* (1736 and 1764), a hat decorated with feathers and with a picture of Duck using a flail, and an old glass goblet.

The house has been called The Charlton Cat since 1921. The crest of the Poore's Arms was a lion rampant and the cat is thought to have been a derisive description of the efforts of the sign artist to depict a lion.

CHARMOUTH, Devon

The Queen's Armes is a long two-storey whitewashed building with a relatively modern slate roof. The Royal Commission on Historic Buildings describes the inn as 'an unusually complete example of a small Medieval House'. There is much original timbering and over the original doorway the initials T.C. are carved in a stone spandrel. These are thought to be the initials of Thomas Chard, one of the Abbots of Forde Abbey. If this is correct, the building must date from the late fifteenth century. It is said that Catherine of Aragon stayed at this inn in 1501 on her journey from Plymouth to marry Prince Arthur who died shortly afterwards. There is much more definite evidence, however, to connect King Charles II with the Queen's Armes. After the Battle of Worcester in 1651 the defeated king travelled north and eventually turned south via Cirencester and Bristol, arriving at Trent House in Dorset where he hid for some days. Meanwhile Captain Ellesdon and Colonel Francis Wyndham journeyed to the Queen's Armes in Charmouth where they met Stephen Limbry who owned a small coasting brig which was to take the king across the Channel. Arrangements were made for Charles to join them at the inn. Meanwhile, Mrs Limbry had become suspicious about the sudden journey to be undertaken by her husband and she locked him in his room when he was making his preparations, threatening to scream the place down if he insisted on carrying out his plan. Charles, who was waiting, was forced to leave the Queen's Armes and strike inland, travelling eastwards towards Salisbury.[11] Eventually he crossed the Channel from the coast of Sussex.

In the years that followed the Restoration, a chapel was set up within the Queen's Armes where nonconformists could worship in peace. John Brice and Bartholomew Westley (as the name was then spelt), the great-grandfather of Charles Wesley, are known to have preached in the inn. In 1661 Westley was imprisoned for refusing to use the common prayer book.

CHELTENHAM, Gloucestershire

The Queen's at the end of the Promenade was built in 1838 on the site of the Sherborne Spa. The architect was Robert William Jearrard who laid out the Lansdowne estate at Cheltenham. The building, of white stucco, is in style a replica of the Temple of Jupiter in Rome. It has four storeys and the façade has a five-bay portico with massive Corinthian pillars which run through the three upper storeys and support a crowning pediment. This is flanked by two four-bay appendages. On the ground floor the windows have semi-circular heads and are set back in deep recesses so that, seen from a distance, there appears to be a long colonnade of rounded arches. Above the ground floor windows are embossed painted crowns with the monogram V.R. The building has often been compared with Russian buildings of the same period (see p 18).

Cheltenham developed rapidly as a spa after George III and his queen came to take the waters, in 1788. The main development to cater for the increasing number of visitors was between 1820 and 1840. The famous Promenade dates from 1825 and the Queen's Hotel provided its climax in 1838.

Detailed descriptions of the Queen's Hotel in early Victorian times are given in J. Goding's *A History of Cheltenham* (1853).

CHERHILL, Wiltshire

The Black Horse, on the north side of the A4, 2 miles east of Calne, is a red-brick building with stone-mullioned windows built by William Catchway between 1765 and 1768 as a posting house. At one time it had a brewhouse but this was demolished in 1939.

Travellers using the inn in its early days were liable to be robbed at night by the Cherhill Gang. One member of the gang is said to have set out on marauding expeditions in summer without a stitch of clothing; not only did such an apparition frighten people on a dark night but a naked man was less easily recognised than one wearing clothes.

The Reverend Plenderleath has left this note about the gang:

> My own uncle who was born in 1776, when he heard of my having accepted a living in Wiltshire, solemnly exhorted me never to think of travelling across the downs without firearms. There was a band of footpads known as the 'Cherhill Gang' who relieved many a traveller of the pence with which he had intended to pay his scores at the Bell or the Black Horse. Two old men who were said to be members of this society lived on into the period of my residence and anyone noticing their venerable white heads bowed over their big prayer books would have taken them for very Village Patriarchs thus ending their simple and blameless lives.

In the days of the Marlborough sheep fairs, the drovers on the way with their flocks used the Black Horse as a resting place. The sheep were penned outside and the drovers slept in the bar.

CHICHESTER, Sussex

The Dolphin and Anchor in West Street, opposite the cathedral, is close to the crossroads marked by the fifteenth-century Market Cross. It has a fine three-storey Georgian frontage with a lettered sign on the parapet which reads 'Dolphin Hotel' and is surmounted by a gilded anchor. The full name results from the amalgamation of two adjoining hostelries in 1910. The Dolphin, which was the larger, was a centre for the Whig party and its fine assembly room is said to have been built by John Abel Smith, MP as a meeting place for his supporters. The Anchor was the headquarters of the Tories. In the seventeenth century both were flourishing posting and coffee houses.

A landlord of the Dolphin, James Ballard, was for a time

Posting Master to Queen Victoria. His widow, who died in 1874, was the last person in Chichester to use a sedan chair.

CHIGWELL, Essex

Ye Olde King's Head on the main road from London to Chelmsford, is an Elizabethan half-timbered building of three storeys and many gables, some of which are large enough to contain rooms. There is a large lattice oriel window on the second floor and latticed bays on the first floor.

Queen Elizabeth I is said to have stayed here for one night and the following morning to have stood on the mounting block by the door where she scuffed and boxed an unlucky page for some neglect of duty. At this period the Forty Day Court or Court of Attachments met at the inn and Verderers Courts were held there until 1855.

Charles Dickens knew 'this delicious old inn near the churchyard' extremely well with its 'overhanging stories, drowsy little panes of glass, and front bulging out and projecting over the pathway'. He made it The Maypole of *Barnaby Rudge* (1840-1). The picture he gives in the novel is as he imagined it must have been in 1775:

> . . . an old building with more gable ends than a lazy man would care to count on a summer day; huge zig-zag chimneys out of which it seemed as though even the smoke could not choose but come in more than naturally fantastic shapes, imparted to it in its tortuous progress . . . Its windows were old diamond paned lattices, its floors were sunken and uneven, its ceilings blackened by the hand of time, and heavy with massive beams.

In the novel, John Willett was the landlord and it was in the panelled room known as the Chester Room (once used as a courtroom) that Mr John Chester met Mr Haredale.

CHIPPENHAM, Wiltshire

The Angel in the Market Place, formerly known as The Bull, is a Georgian coaching inn of three stories surmounted by a balustrade. The porch, also with balustrade, is supported by Tuscan columns. Tobias Smollett tells us that Peregrine Pickle's mother served in the Angel as a chambermaid so the inn must have flourished before 1751 when his novel was published. An issue of the *Bath Journal* in 1774 contains this notice from the proprietor:

> It having been found that the other Inns were not sufficient for Properly Accommodating the Nobility and Gentry Travelling through this Town, occasioned by the great Increase thereof arising from the NEW ROAD
>
> THE ANGEL INN
>
> is just now fitted up in a neat and convenient Manner; where the Gentlemen and Ladies who will be so good as to use this House will meet with the most obliging Treatment and reasonable usage
>
> From their very humble servant
>
> THOMAS STROUD

The Angel was an important coaching house and its bow window gave a good view both ways so that the staff might see coaches approaching.

In the parliamentary election of 1875, Sir John Neeld of Grittleton, who was a Conservative candidate, had his committee room at the Angel Inn. When the result was declared in his favour there was a riot in the town and rowdy scenes outside the inn. Windows were broken and the landlord climbed to the top floor and threw bottles at the crowd beneath.

CHIPPERFIELD, Hertfordshire

The Two Brewers facing Chipperfield Green existed in the late seventeenth century as a village alehouse within the manor of King's Langley. Houses on either side have been added since World War II. One was previously a grocer's shop; the other housed the schoolmaster. The building is of brick with red-tiled roof and a plaster and colour-washed front to which bay windows have been added. The post sign which stands on the green opposite the inn carries the usual picture of two men carrying a barrel of strong beer slung from a pole, the ends of which rest on their shoulders.

In the nineteenth century the Two Brewers was used as

training quarters where bare-fist fighters prepared for their bouts. Bob Fitzsimmons, Jem Mace (champion in 1861) and Tom Sayers (champion in 1857) sparred in the old club room behind the main building and took training runs round Chipperfield Common. The inn became a mecca for enthusiasts from miles around who drove to the inn to see the champions at work.

In those days the inn had large stables as former landlords farmed the adjoining land and provided overnight accommodation for hunters brought from a distance to follow the local foxhounds. The original tap-room is now part of the lounge in which there is a large open fireplace spanned by a finely carved oak beam.

CHIPPING NORTON, Oxfordshire

The White Hart in the High Street may well have origins in the fourteenth century for the town was an important wool centre in the days of Richard II. The painted wall sign bears his badge. The oldest parts of the present stone-built inn are Tudor but the three-storey frontage of mellow stone dates from 1811. The original wings formed a galleried courtyard but although the stone stairs which led to it may still be seen, the gallery has long since been enclosed. In one room inside the inn there is floor to ceiling Elizabethan panelling and some Tudor fireplaces may be seen.

Behind the inn is Diston's Lane. William Diston was a landlord of the White Hart in the 1660s. He issued trade tokens from the inn in 1666. Diston must have been a fairly wealthy man for a few years previously he is said to have paid a ransom of £6,000 for his uncle, Henry Cornish, who had been taken prisoner by Royalists.

Chipping Norton became an important coaching centre towards the end of the eighteenth century; all the through coaches from London to Cheltenham or Worcester inned at the White Hart.

CLIFTON HAMPDEN, Oxfordshire

The Barley Mow in this village is on the south bank of the

Thames and actually in the parish of Long Wittenham in Berkshire. It is just over 3 miles east of Abingdon. The old building of timber and thatch dates from 1350 and looks to be little more than a country cottage. The curved tree trunks or 'crucks' which provide the frame for the walls can still be seen at the gable end. The low timbered ceilings inside cause all but the very shortest customers to stoop.

It was from the windows of the Barley Mow that Jerome K. Jerome must have watched the river, for it was here that he wrote much of his *Three Men in a Boat* (1889).

CLOVELLY, Devon

The New Inn in Steep Street which descends by steps to the harbour of this little fishing village on the North Devon coast was largely rebuilt after World War I yet it rises from the cobbles as though it had always been fused into the rocky hillside. It is a typical North Devon building with grey tiles and whitewashed walls and has catered for visitors for over 100 years.

In 1890, Sir Walter Raleigh, who later became the first Professor of English Literature at Oxford, spent his honeymoon at the New Inn from which he wrote to his sister, Jessie:

> We are married and safely at Clovelly. We live in a little room in the garden hanging above the rest of the inn, where we hope to stay a week . . . Opposite my balcony here is an alcove where my friend the Dean sat and drank cider and gallivanted with a little waiting maid, niece of the proprietor, whom he ungratefully called 'baggage'.

COBHAM, Kent

The Leather Bottle is a seventeenth-century half-timbered inn noted for its associations with Charles Dickens; the sign which shows Mr Pickwick standing on a chair addressing the club, makes this clear to the passer-by. Fifty years ago the timbers were plastered over.[12] Dickens knew the inn well for he used it for a scene in *Pickwick Papers* (1836-7), Tracy Tupman fled to the Leather Bottle after he had been jilted by

Rachael Wardle. In a letter to Mr Pickwick he wrote 'Any letter addressed to me at the Leather Bottle, Cobham, Kent, will be forwarded, supposing I still exist'. After receiving the letter, Mr Pickwick set out for this 'clean and commodious village alehouse' with Winkle and Snodgrass and found Tracy Tupman consoling himself with bacon, roast fowl and ale. They all stayed the night and next day departed on the coach to London.

Dickens constantly visited the Leather Bottle and in 1841 stayed there overnight with his biographer, John Forster. Later when Dickens was living at Gadshill Place, little more than 3 miles from Cobham, he often took his friends there and one of his favourite walks, according to Forster was 'round Cobham, skirting the park and village and passing the Leather Bottle'.

COLCHESTER, Essex

The Red Lion in the High Street of this old Roman town of Camulodunum is on the site of a Roman building; mosaic pavements were found during excavations in the yard in 1882. There is early fifteenth-century masonry in the cellars and parts of the present building reveal the wattle and daub structure of 1470 when it was the private house of a wealthy burgess. The house became an inn early in the sixteenth century when it was licensed as a 'wyn tavern' and considerable extensions were made. The frontage is timbered with projecting upper storeys and the woodwork is finely carved (see p 35). There are traceried panels beneath the windows of the upper floors and the spandrels of the arched Tudor doorway have fifteenth-century carving depicting St George and the Dragon. Inside there are massive moulded beams with carved brackets, and much timber has been revealed which, in Victorian times, was hidden behind facings.

Throughout the sixteenth century the inn was known as Le Whyght Lyon but by 1625 had become the Red Lion. It is possible that the colour-change was made to commemorate the Union of the Crowns in 1604.

In 1648 when Colchester fell after a siege by the Parliamentarians, the Royalist garrison was rounded up by Thomas

Fairfax in the yard of the Red Lion and the defending leaders, Sir George Lisle and Sir Charles Lucas were taken out and shot outside the castle.

In the years that followed the inn twice issued its own trade tokens, in 1656 under a landlord called Rich, and in 1668 under Richard Boyer. In the eighteenth century the coaching trade flourished. In 1756 an express service to London was inaugurated at the Red Lion though another inn, The Cups, on the opposite side of the street, was then the major inn. In the entrance to the Red Lion yard, now covered in, is a rainwater head dated 1716, a range of brass service bells and a fine old Parliament clock.

The Marquis of Granby Inn at No 24 North Hill was built in 1520 and has some particularly fine sixteenth-century timbering in the east wing including a carved beam with stylised leaves and animals which rests on brackets with carved human figures. The inn was extensively restored in 1914. The Marquis of Granby appears on the building as a wall sign in a plaster cartouche. John Manners, Marquis of Granby, was the eldest son of the 3rd Duke of Rutland. He was British Commander-in-Chief in Germany during the Seven Years War. One day the marquis was about to lead a cavalry charge against the enemy when his wig fell off. His aide-de-campe drew his attention to the fact. 'Damn the wig' cried the marquis 'I can charge baldheaded'. He had a warm feeling towards the men under his command and many of his officers who were disabled were helped by the marquis to establish themselves as innkeepers. Hence the frequency of 'Marquis of Granby' inns.

COLNBROOK, Buckinghamshire

The Ostrich Inn in the High Street is on the old London to Bath road, 17 miles from Hyde Park Corner. It was founded as a hospice in 1106 by Milo Crispin, in trust to the Abbey of Abingdon, 'for the good of travellers'. The name of the inn is thought to be a corruption of the word 'hospice': earlier versions were 'Ospringe, Ostridge and Oastriche.[13]

In the thirteenth century Thomas Cole, a clothier from Reading, frequently stayed at the inn on his way to London. John

Page 53: *(above)* The Angel and Royal, Grantham; *(below)* The Black Swan, Helmsley

Page 54: *(above)* The Sir John Falstaff, Higham ; *(below)* the yard of The George, Huntingdon

Jarman the innkeeper, and his wife, who already had a reputation for stealing from guests, prepared a bed for Cole which could be tipped so that its occupant would slide through a trap door head first into a cauldron of hot liquid in the kitchen below. Three times the scheme misfired when Cole decided to change his plans at the last moment; the fourth time Cole died but when his body was later found in the brook the culprits were traced and hanged.[14]

King John is said to have stopped at the Ostrich on his way to Runnymede to sign the Magna Carta and Jean Froissart, the medieval chronicler, tells us that ambassadors who had been to dine with Edward III 'after they departed lay the same night at Colnbrook'. When the Black Prince returned from Europe in 1355 with his prisoner King John of France, he is said to have been met by his father, Edward III, at the Ostrich. It was certainly a well known inn where visitors to Windsor often called to clean up and change their clothes before proceeding to an audience.

The present Ostrich, which dates from early in the sixteenth century, is built of timber and brick with a double gable and at one time had a galleried yard. Queen Elizabeth stayed here in 1558 on a night when bad road conditions prevented her from reaching Windsor.

In 1649 when Charles I had been taken to London to stand trial at Westminster Hall, Captain Fanshawe and John Dowcett were on their way towards London to meet a messenger who was to bring them news of the king. Seeing a man riding west, they assumed him to be the messenger they were expecting. He asked Fanshawe and Dowcett to come with him to the Ostrich Inn and when the small party arrived the Royalists were overpowered and locked up as prisoners. Shortly afterwards, however, Lord Richmond arrived with a group of Royalist supporters, carrying the message. Realising what had happened he threatened to set fire to the Ostrich; there was a short but fierce fight, and Fanshawe and Dowcett were released. During the Civil War the Ostrich was for a short time the base used by Prince Rupert before he faced the Londoners at Brentford. In 1657 Samuel Mills, the landlord of the inn, issued a trade token.

In the early eighteenth century there is, almost inevitably, a story of Dick Turpin, though this is more likely to be true than most of the stories about him for Hounslow Heath was notorious at this time for highway robberies. Turpin is said to have been pursued to the inn by the Bow Street runners and, realising his danger, leapt from his bedroom window, mounted his horse, and rode away, successfully avoiding capture.

No doubt the Ostrich had some share in the coaching trade of the eighteenth and nineteenth centuries but **The George** on the same street was then more important as a coaching inn.

CORFE CASTLE, Dorset

The Greyhound lies close to the gap in the chalk ridge of the Purbeck Hills through which the A351 finds its way from Wareham to Swanage. It is at the northern end of the village at the foot of the hill on which stand the ruins of Corfe Castle, one of the last Royalist strongholds during the Civil War. The inn is of whitewashed Purbeck stone with a slate roof carrying dormer windows. The entrance porch is pillared and supports a small room. Throughout the coaching era the Greyhound was a useful stop on the route to Swanage.

Thomas Hardy knew this inn well. He used the name of Corvsgate for Corfe in his novels *Desperate Remedies* (1871) and *The Hand of Ethelberta* (1876).

CORSHAM, Wiltshire

The Methuen Arms has a Georgian façade with a pillared porch which dates from 1805 but behind this frontage is a Tudor building which became The Red Lion c1608. This was previously Wintners Court and belonged to the Nott family. In 1732 Elizabeth Webber, a widowed member of the family, became the owner and the inn then passed in turn to her daughter, Christian. Perhaps the initials and date C.W. 1749 carved on a wall, date from her time. When she died, the Red Lion passed to the Methuen family. There was then more rebuilding (1805) and the sign was changed to bear the arms of Lord Methuen.

The stone doorposts of the main entrance carry the traditional chequers design used by tavern-keepers who were also money-changers.

CRANBROOK, Kent

The George in Stone Street existed as an inn in Tudor times when Cranbrook was a flourishing woollen town. The accommodation was regarded as fine enough to meet the needs of Queen Elizabeth I who came to the town in 1575 to see how the weaving was done. There is a story that she walked into Cranbrook along a mile of Kentish broadcloth but no doubt the distance has been exaggerated over the years. From the street the inn now shows little sign of its real age. The long frontage with a tile-hung second storey with delicate wrought-iron balcony, and the steeply pitched roof with dormer windows, all date from late Georgian times when the house became an important coaching inn. Inside, however, are heavy old moulded beams, open fireplaces, a very fine early eighteenth-century balustered staircase (c1705) and very extensive cellars.

The magistrates' court was held in an upper room of the George for about 300 years and did not move to new quarters until 1859. In the seventeenth century witches and warlocks were brought to the court for examination before being committed to the Maidstone Sessions. French prisoners were probably tried here for they appear to have been chained to a strong heavy beam in the floor. Remains of irons have been found and what appeared to be initials with the date 1760 were found on a corridor ceiling.

CRAWLEY, Sussex

The George is noted for its gallows sign which has spanned the High Street since Regency days. When the coaching trade flourished an extension to the inn was built on an island site in the middle of the main road and the sign was erected to link the two parts. The original building was a private house which became an inn in 1615. This is the date on a massive stone fireplace with fine moulding and sunk spandrels to be seen in the hall. The roof is of Horsham stone slabs but the front which is tile-hung on the upper storey, is relatively late, as is the chimney.

The George was a half-way house on the coaching route through Reigate which formed the Brighton Road. The Prince Regent first changed horses here on a journey from Carlton House to Brighton in 1783 and later became a frequent visitor. In 1789 the inn was the subject of a drawing by Thomas Rowlandson.

Soon after Queen Victoria came to the throne as many as fifty coaches changed horses at the George every twenty-four hours. Even when the railway came the decline was relatively slow for amateur coachmen and sportsmen still used the inn as a port of call on record-breaking runs.

The George was closely associated with prize fighters such as Tom Sayers and Pedlar Palmer who took part in contests on Crawley Down but rather more people will know it as the inn where Belcher trained boy Jim for his fight against Crab Wilson in Sir Arthur Conan Doyle's novel *Rodney Stone* (1896).

DARTFORD, Kent

The Royal Victoria and Bull in the High Street began as a hospice attached to the Augustinian Priory of St Mary and St Margaret. It is on the old Watling Street and was probably where Canterbury pilgrims journeying from London spent their first night. At this time, Urban Baldock, the landlord, and a member of parliament, was a friend of Geoffrey Chaucer. In 1508 the house is described in a rent roll of the priory lands as Le Hole Bole with a rent of 40 shillings (£2) a year. Part of the present building is Elizabethan though portions of earlier walls may well have been incorporated.

The Bull was at one time a galleried inn with a large courtyard. Changes were made in the eighteenth century when it became a busy coaching inn and the fine Georgian façade with its high windows was built with a central portico which leads to the courtyard (now covered in). Remains of the old wooden galleries may still be seen.

An incident in 1775 concerned a doctor, John Parker, who, when seeking to evade responsibility for his debts, stayed at the Bull. A certain Joseph Stackpole arrived at the inn with a bailiff who was told to take Parker and lock him up. Parker, in anger, threatened the bailiff with a pistol and one of his friends extinguished the lights. Stackpole went to the rescue but Parker's friends seized him, a carbine he was carrying exploded and Parker was killed. Was it by accident or intent? Stackpole faced a murder trial at Maidstone and it was two years before the case was settled: the court finally decided that Parker died as a result of an accident.

Richard Trevithick, the Cornish engineer, died at the Bull in 1833.

DEVIZES, Wiltshire

The Bear in the Market Place was an inn at the end of the sixteenth century for there is a record that a certain John Sawter applied for a licence in 1599. Some claim that Queen Elizabeth halted at the inn in 1574 when travelling from Bath to Lacock.

Traces of the old inn still exist but the frontage is mainly Georgian. The right wing is the earlier and has the entrance, a porch supporting a bear holding a bunch of grapes. The name of the hotel extends as a lettered sign right across this part of the façade. The later wing to the left is of solid stone blocks (see p 35).

The Bear was one of the most fashionable coaching inns of the eighteenth century. There were many notable landlords. In the early eighteenth century the owner, John Watts, lived in the inn and acted as host. He sold it to John Child, a local grocer and brother of Sir Francis Child, a London banker who was active locally as a Tory. In 1754 the Bear was rented by John Turner, a Land Tax Receiver, who paid an annual rent of £48 10s 6d (£48.52½). Then came George Whatley. During his tenancy weekly meetings of local townsmen were held in the inn and this led to the formation of the Devizes Bear Club. The most interesting tenant, however, was Thomas Lawrence who came to the Bear in 1772 from the White Lion and American Coffee House in Bristol—where the Grand Hotel now stands. He was the father of sixteen children. Fanny Burney describes a 'long visit' she made with Mrs Thrale while the Lawrence family was at the Bear.

> The house was full of books, as well as paintings, drawings and music: and all the family seem not only ingenious and industrious, but amiable; added to which they are strikingly handsome.

They were particularly impressed by the son, Thomas:

> . . . a most lovely boy of ten years of age, who seems to be not merely the wonder of their family, but of the times, for his astonishing skill in drawing. They protest he has never had any instruction, yet showed us some of his productions that were really beautiful. Those that were copies were delightful—those of his own composition amazing, though far inferior. I was equally struck by the boy and his works. We found that he had been taken to town, and that all the painters had been very kind to him, and Sir Joshua Reynolds had pronounced him, the mother said, the most promising genius he had ever met.

Very shortly after this the Lawrence family left the Bear, and in 1779 young Thomas Lawrence started to work at a studio in Bath and soon became the main support of the family. He was to become the greatest portrait painter of his time.[15] In 1815 he was knighted and in 1820 became President of the Royal Academy.

Many eighteenth-century notabilities used the Bear which was on the main route to fashionable Bath. These included Jane Austen, Samuel Foote, David Garrick, Dr Johnson, Sir Joshua Reynolds, Richard Brinsley Sheridan, Sarah Siddons and John Wilkes.

George Long in his book *English Inns and Roadhouses* (1937) refers to a scratched sentence on a window in the inn which read:

> John Blome, Mircht, on his way from London to Bath for execution, february 23rd, 1766.

Apparently the condemned man with his escort had arrived in Devizes too late for the town lock-up to be used and they were obliged to stay in the inn.

Other visitors have included George III and Queen Charlotte who stayed at the Bear on 16 September 1789, King Edward VII as Prince of Wales when he visited Devizes in 1893 to review the Wiltshire Yeomanry, Prince Arthur of Connaught, and Prince Edward of Saxe Weimar.

DORCHESTER, Dorset

The King's Arms in High East Street was mentioned in an Assessment of 1737. By 1783 it had become an established coaching inn on the London to Exeter Road. It was here that George III changed horses when passing through Dorchester on his way to Melcombe Regis, or Weymouth as we know it today. The three-storey frontage has two large semi-circular bays above a pillared portico and to the left is the arched entrance to the yard with a balcony on the first floor above. An armorial bracket sign hangs high above the street between the first and second floors.

The King's Arms has had many notable visitors. Admiral Lord Nelson and Sir Thomas Masterman Hardy, Kitchener of Khartoum and, of course, Thomas Hardy who used the present hotel lounge as the scene for the entertainment given by Michael Henchard, the Mayor of Casterbridge, to his friends. Hardy's novel *The Mayor of Casterbridge* was published in 1886.

Edward VII when Prince of Wales stayed at the hotel in 1856 and the Sheffield plate used at his table is displayed in the Casterbridge Lounge as it is now called.

DORCHESTER-ON-THAMES, Oxfordshire

The George was once the hospice of a priory founded in 1140. Dorchester was an important centre in Roman times and from the seventh to the ninth centuries was the cathedral city of Wessex and later of Mercia. The great abbey church still dominates the town. The George lies opposite the abbey and dates, in part, from about 1450.

In the eighteenth century it became an important coaching house on the route from London to Oxford. The building retains many historic features. Behind the inn can be seen the old galleried 'lodgings' reached by a staircase, perhaps the earliest of its kind in the country. Many of the inn rooms are timbered and the dining room with its great fireplace is very little changed since it was the abbey monk's brewhouse.

When the coaching trade declined in the nineteenth century the inn almost lost its identity. Parts were converted into a private house and the landlord set up a wheelwrights's shop in the yard.

DORKING, Surrey

The White Horse in the High Street is a two-storey black-and-white building with a long frontage broken by three gables and a central coaching entrance. The oldest parts are sixteenth century but the origins of the inn are thirteenth century. A building on the site was granted to the Knights Templars by William, Earl Warenne of Surrey and later, in 1278, it passed into the holding of the Knights Hospitallers of St John of Jerusalem. The badge of the Templars was a white cross and the house was known as Cross House. The present name—White Horse—almost certainly derives from White Cross.

The oldest part of the present timbered building dates from c1520 when it was used as a vicarage. In 1531 it was surrendered to George Rolle, gentleman, and was known as Rolle's Tenement until it became the White Horse Inn in 1750. Much rebuilding was done to meet the needs of the coaching trade. In 1793 it is recorded that the Brighton coach stopped regularly at the White Horse for passengers to take a meal. In the 1830s the landlord was William Penn who claimed descent from the founder of Pennsylvania. At this period the inn became a favourite resort of invalids in the summer season.

The cellars have been cut from solid sandstone and are probably the oldest part of the house. In 1936 a fine eighteenth-century staircase was installed.

DUNSTER, Somerset

The Luttrell Arms in the village High Street close to the seventeenth-century yarn market, is said to have been a guest house of the abbots of Cleeve whose Cistercian monastery, now in ruins, is about 4 miles distant. It is a three-storey stone structure with a porch tower that was either built or materially altered between 1622 and 1629 (see p 36). The core is a fifteenth-century Gothic hall which is now divided by a floor into two parts. The upper chamber contains a fine hammer-beam roof, and the lower chamber, which was once the inn kitchen, is now a bar.

The building is known to have been an inn called The Ship in 1651. By that time the influence of the Luttrell family had manifested itself. Some of the rooms contain seventeenth-century plaster work. The finest example is a tall overmantel which carries the arms of England and France and a panel showing Actaeon in the form of a stag being torn to pieces by his hounds on Mount Cithaeron. A male figure in a triangle may represent James I or the lord of the castle—George Luttrell. The Ship became the Luttrell Arms in 1779 in compliment to Hugh Luttrell whose family had been the lords of the manor since 1404.

DYMCHURCH, Kent

The Ship is an old brick-built inn facing St Mary's Bay on the coast of the English Channel and is backed by Romney Marsh. It was thus an ideal centre for smugglers at a time when a licence was needed for the export of wool. There was an illicit trade with the continent and smugglers would bring over kegs of brandy and take back bales of wool. The Ship had a number of secret stairways and hiding places and several tracks ran inland from this stretch of coast through desolate country to isolated villages and inns on the northern fringe of the marsh. The smugglers knew the country intimately and this explained their success in evading the attempts of the authorities to suppress the traffic in contraband which continued well into the nineteenth century.

The New Hall, where the justices met, is close to the inn and the church. This is where the Lords, Bailiff and Jurats of Romney Marsh hold their annual Grand Leth at Whitsuntide, adjourning afterwards to the Ship Hotel for a meal to celebrate the occasion. The main course of this meal is always Romney Marsh lamb.

The sign of the Ship over the main doorway is an unusual one. It consists of a large carved and gilded medallion showing a sailing ship at sea within a wreath of laurel leaves.

ESHER, Surrey

The Bear on the A3 was established in 1529 but there is little to see of the early structure: the stucco frontage is probably early nineteenth century and the interior has been completely modernised. In coaching days it was an important posting house at the start of the second stage from London to Portsmouth and it had stabling for a hundred horses. At that time it was known as the Brown Bear and today there are effigy signs in the form of two brown bears on the parapet described by Charles Harper as 'squatting on their rumps and stroking their stomachs in a manner strongly suggestive of repletion or indigestion'. The Bear has associations with Claremont, the near-by house built by Robert Clive in 1786, now a girls' school. In 1816 Claremont became the home of Princess Charlotte when she married Prince Leopold of Saxe-Coburg, though she died a year later. In 1831, the prince became King of the Belgians and in 1832 married the eldest daughter of Louis-Philippe, King of the French. During the revolution of 1848, Louis-Philippe left Paris and came to England and his son-in-law placed Claremont at his disposal. Members of the French royal household were accommodated at the Brown Bear, and in a glass case in the entrance hall are the heavy leather jackboots worn by the postboy who drove the fugitive Louis-Philippe to his new home at Claremont.

FARNHAM, Surrey

The Jolly Farmer at the foot of Firgrove Hill was the birthplace of William Cobbett in 1762. His father not only kept the inn but also farmed the nearby lands. Cobbett himself wrote that he was 'born in the farmhouse, bred up at the ploughtail, with a smock frock on my back, taking delight in all the pursuits of the farmers, liking their society and having among them my most esteemed friends'. The inn building shows too distinct periods: the right-hand timbered and gabled wing is sixteenth century, the rest is seventeenth century. The garden behind the inn is described by Cobbett:

> From my very infancy from the age of six years, when I climbed up the side of a steep sand rock, and there scooped me out a plot of four feet square to make me a garden, and the soil for which I carried up in the bosom of my little blue smock frock, I have never lost one particle of my passion for these healthy and rational, and heart-warming pursuits.

He also tells how he viewed this little plot in later life:

> The post-boy going downhill, and not a bad road, whisked me in a few minutes to the Bush Inn, from the garden of which I could see the prodigious sand-hill where I had begun my gardening works.

The Bush Inn mentioned by Cobbett, now **The Bush Hotel,** dates mainly from the sixteenth century and, after some re-building, became an important coaching inn in Georgian times. It was probably The Shrub of Edna Lyall's novels.

FITTLEWORTH, Sussex

The Swan is a fifteenth-century country inn which became a posting house in the eighteenth century. It is stone built and the upper storey is hung with red tiles. The roof was once covered with slabs of Horsham stone but only nine rows remain; the rest is covered with red tiles. The old stables are now used for storage and the iron hay-racks are attached to the front of the inn as flower baskets.

John Constable stayed at the Swan when he came to Fittle-worth on painting expeditions with his brewer namesake. The inn has always attracted artists and students of art. The residents' lounge to the left of the main entrance, sometimes called the 'picture room', has many oil paintings framed as panels around the walls. They include pictures signed by S. C. Burgess, R. H. Shapman, H. E. Cheesman, H. Clarke, H. C. Clifford, G. Constable, E. Edward, C. Farmer, Mary Harding, E. Holland, E. Knight, F. Litchford, Stuart Lloyd, F. J. Neale, A. C. Osborne, L. S. Palmer, C. Pretorious, R. Rachley, E. Handley

Read, W. E. Searle, A. Trotter, W. B. Watson, A. W. Weedon and G. Whelpton.

In the hall is an old inn sign, Ye Swanne Inne, painted about 1900 by R. Caton Woodville. This was lost for many years but turned up mysteriously at an auction sale in Haslemere and was returned to the inn. The original sign depicted a nude figure with a striking likeness to Queen Victoria, sitting astride a swan. This was soon altered. The face was changed and diaphanous drapes were painted in to transform the figure into a fairy queen The reverse side of the sign shows the swan with a ring round its neck and a frog smoking a pipe in a floating tankard. The bar has a fine collection of old truncheons.

Until a few years ago the inn had a gallows sign but road widening led to its removal. The present sign incorporates the coats of arms of His Grace, the Duke of Norfolk, The Lord of the Manor of Bury, and of Lord Leconfield, Lord of the Manors of Stopham, Waltham and Amberley.

FOREST OF DEAN, Gloucestershire

The Speech House, known as The King's Lodge until 1801, is near Coleford in the centre of the Forest of Dean. It is a square, grey-sandstone building of three storeys which stands roughly 600ft above sea level. It has always been a Verderers' Court and is said to be the oldest court of law in England.[16] The site was previously occupied by a building called Kenesley where the ancient Speech Court was held, but in 1670 a warrant was issued for a new and larger building. This was completed c1674 and the stables in 1676. A stone lintel believed to be from the stables is now to be seen over one of the entrances. Much of the building, including the west front, is in its original state and here, over the entrance to the court room, there is a weathered escutcheon in stone with the date 1680 and the initials 'C.R.II'. The court room with its ancient roof beams is now the hotel dining room, but it is still officially opened from time to time to deal with matters of 'vert and venison' though this is now little more than a formality. At one time the court could condemn a man to death. Today, the local magistrates normally deal with 'vert' offences and as there are now no deer in the forest, venison offences do not arise. At one time the court room in Speech House was divided by rails into compartments for the jury and accused. Today there is only a low raised oak gallery or daïs to remind one of its functions as a court.

Speech House was first let as an inn in the 1860s; it was enlarged in 1883.

FYFIELD, Berkshire

The White Hart on the A420 between Faringdon and Oxford, is a half-timbered tiled building which dates back to the fifteenth century. The Lord of the Manor was Sir John Golafre and when he died in 1442 he left enough money to build and endow a hospital or chantry house for the poor to be run by a priest who would pray for the soul of the founder. (Sir John's monument may be seen in Fyfield Church.) In 1580, after the dissolution of the monasteries, the house was purchased by St John's College, Oxford, which already owned land in the vicinity, and was then leased to tenants who kept it as a tavern. The original hall of the hospital was divided into two floors.

In 1963 the college restored the original hall with its arch-braced roof and also the chantry room to their original state. The property was then re-let for use as an inn.

GLASTONBURY, Somerset

The George and Pilgrims is one of the few remaining medieval inns in England. It was built by Abbot John de Selwood in 1475 as a *novum hospitium* for pilgrims to the Benedictine abbey, now in ruins. Many pilgrims received free board and lodging in the abbey hospice; the Pilgrims Inn, as it was called before it became the George, was for more important middle-class guests and visitors. The freestone building has suffered little (see p 36). There is a central archway and the three-storey bays on either side have mullioned windows, cusped and glazed, though partly filled in with solid stone in the two upper storeys. Above the entrance are three carved shields. One shows the armorial bearings of the abbey, the second bears the arms of Edward IV and the third still awaits the arms of the patron builder. The initials of this builder 'I.S.' can be found on shields in the cornices. To the left of the entrance is a stone column which once supported a massive corbel holding a bracket clock and later the sign.[17]

A long flagged and timbered hallway runs through the inn and, to the left of the entrance, massive vertical pieces of hewn timber form the wall between this hallway and the parlour where the abbot received his guests. This room has been enlarged to take in the old abbot's kitchen but the original fireplace has gone. There are, however, many interesting eighteenth century delft tiles on the wall behind the present fireplace. Among them is one more recent tile: the clue to its identification is clear enough but most people usually take some time to find it.

A spiral staircase leads to the hotel bedrooms and eight of them have fifteenth-century features. They have been named after famous local churchmen. From one of them Henry VIII is said to have watched the burning of Glastonbury Abbey in 1539.

GLOUCESTER

The New Inn was built about 1445 by John Twyning, a monk of the Abbey of St Peter, on the site of a smaller hospice, to accommodate the increasing number of pilgrims flocking to the shrine of King Edward II who had been barbarously murdered in Berkeley Castle in 1327. At first no one was anxious to bury the body but the Abbey of Gloucester risked the anger of the Queen and entombed Edward in the church.

There is no formal frontage to the New Inn. It is approached through an archway leading to the old courtyard which has an open gallery at first-floor level. It was on this balcony in Tudor times that the audiences gathered to watch the theatrical performances given by itinerant players in the courtyard below. Lady Jane Grey was proclaimed queen from the gallery on 9 July 1552. Ten days later the usurpation was over and she was imprisoned in the Tower of London.

GODMANSTONE, Dorset

The Smith's Arms on the A352 between Dorchester and Cerne

Abbas is reputed to be the smallest licensed house in England. It is a fifteenth-century building of knapped flints and stone with a deep thatch. A fine sign showing a smith working at an anvil rises above the timber porch. The inn was once a black-smith's shop and is said to have been granted a licence by Charles II who stopped to have his horse shod and asked for a drink. 'I have no licence, sire', said the blacksmith. Then and there the king granted him one.

GODSTOW, Oxfordshire

The Trout is a stone-built country inn on the bank of the Thames about 3 miles north-west of the city of Oxford. It was originally a hospice attached to the Benedictine nunnery at Godstow, founded by Dame Ediva of Winchester c1138. (Young Rosamond Clifford, daughter of Walter, Lord Clifford, who was a mistress of Henry II at Woodstock, ended her days in the nunnery in 1176.) After the dissolution of the monasteries the nunnery became a private house which was destroyed by Thomas Fairfax in 1646. The hospice was then enlarged to become an inn using building stone from the nunnery ruins.

For years the Trout has been a noted meeting place for the undergraduates and staff of Oxford University, particularly those addicted to boating. The interior has many early features —stone fireplaces, panelling and fine beams.

It was on the stretch of water seen from the terrace of the Trout that Lewis Carroll (Charles Lutwidge Dodgson), on the afternoon of 4 July 1862, first told the story of *Alice in Wonderland* (1865) to three small girls during a river trip. The party also included Robin Duckworth (later to become Dean of Westminster) and one of his friends.

GORING-ON-THAMES, Oxfordshire

Ye Miller of Mansfield is a creeper-covered hotel built of flint and brick standing near the bridge over the Thames. The miller of Mansfield was the first landlord. Accounts vary as to whether his name was Richard or John Cockell and whether the king who provided the land for the inn was Henry II or Henry III. The story, however, is always the same. Cockell was a miller.

He entertained the king, who had become separated from his company during a hunting foray in Sherwood Forest. Unaware of the identity of his guest, the miller gave him a pie containing venison from a deer poached in the forest. He asked the king what was in the pie. The old ballad continued the story in these words:

> 'Then I think' quoth our King 'that it's venison';
> 'Eche Foole', quoth Richard, 'full that you may see:
> Never are we without two or three in the roof
> Very well fleshed and excellent fat:
> But I pray thee say nothing where'er thou go;
> We would not for two pence the King should know.'

When the company found the king next morning it soon became obvious to the miller who his guest had been and he was filled with anguish. However, grateful for the hospitality, the king pardoned him and gave Cockell some land at Goring on which to build the tavern which became Ye Miller of Mansfield.

GRANTHAM, Lincolnshire

The Angel and Royal, known simply as The Angel until 1866, is one of the oldest and most historic inns in England. It stands on ground believed to have belonged to the Knights Templars until their order was dissolved in 1312. For at least a hundred years before this date there must have been a hostelry here where royal travellers, merchants and pilgrims were entertained. Tradition says that King John and his train of courtiers lodged here on 23 February 1213 when he held a court, two years before the signing of Magna Carta. The hostelry appears to have passed to the Knights Hospitallers c1312 and the cellars and a few of the old thick walls may date from this period. The entrance archway is believed to have been built in Edward III's reign. Heads of King Edward and Queen Phillipa of Hainault are carved on its hood moulding. The rest of the front of the inn was built in the fifteenth century. Above the gateway is a carved and gilded angel holding a crown of the conventional leaf design common in church decoration (see p 53).

The upper room, above the archway, known for centuries

Page 71: *(above)* The George and Dragon, Hurstbourne Tarrant; *(right)* The Duke's Head, King's Lynn

Page 72: *(above)* The Swan, Lavenham ; *(below)* The Bull, Long Melford

as the State Room, or *La Chambre du Roi,* was used by King Richard III on 19 October 1483. It was here that he wrote a letter to the Lord Chancellor bidding him send the Great Seal so that he might proclaim the treachery of his cousin the Second Duke of Buckingham. A facsimile of this letter is in the British Museum and a photograph of it hangs in the State Room. The room has an oriel window over the gateway and two other windows, each with carved stone ceilings. Another window in the hotel has a carving of a 'pelican of piety' feeding her young with her own blood. This has a religious origin and supports the view that the house may have been used by pilgrims to the Shrine of St Wulfram, to whom the parish church is dedicated.

Little is known of the history of the Angel between 1500 and 1700 except that King Charles I visited the inn on 17 May 1633. In 1706 when the landlord, Michael Soloman, died, he left a legacy of 40s (£2) a year in his will to be paid for the preaching of an annual sermon against drunkenness each Michaelmas Day.

In the eighteenth century the Angel became one of the foremost coaching and posting inns on the Great North Road: hundreds of coaches pulled up outside every week including the York, Edinburgh and Aberdeen Royal Mail, the Queen Charlotte bound for Edinburgh, the York and Leeds Post Coach and the York Highflyers. There was a good deal of new building at this period including the wings which enclose the yard. Four square rainwaterheads bear the date 1746 and the device of a griffin. The Angel continued to prosper even after the advent of the railways in the nineteenth century. In 1857 the landlord, Richard John Boyall, inserted an announcement in the guide of the Great Northern Railway thanking 'the nobility and the Public generally' for so liberally patronising his hotel.

The Prince of Wales (later Edward VII) visited the Angel in 1866 when it became the Angel and Royal.

The Beehive is a little inn in Castlegate noted for its 'living' sign. A lime tree grows from the roadside gutter and on a platform among its branches is a beehive which the bees can be seen to enter and leave. Between the tree and the inn a small signboard bears this verse:

Stop traveller, this wondrous sign explore
And say, when thou has viewed it O'er and o'er;
Grantham, now two rarities are there
A lofty steeple and a living sign.

GRASMERE, Westmorland

The Swan lies on the A591 north of Grasmere Village and was a posting house used before the horses began the steady ascent of Dunmail Raise. It was frequently visited by William Wordsworth who wrote:

Who does not know the famous Swan
Object uncouth, and yet our boast,
For it was painted by the host,
His own conceit the figure planned,
'Twas coloured all by his own hand.

The host referred to in this verse was Anthony Wilson, a friend of the poet Coleridge. Other painters to tackle the sign of the Swan at Grasmere have included S. Garside and Margaret Summer.

The inn was used by Sir Walter Scott in 1805.

GRETA BRIDGE, Yorkshire

The Morritt Arms, formerly the seventeenth-century George, is an old stone-built coaching inn which provided hospitality for Charles Dickens and Hablot Browne when they arrived by coach in deep snow on 31 January 1838. This was the end of a two-day journey from London on the Carlisle coach. They stayed at the Morritt Arms and continued their journey later by poste-chaise to Barnard Castle (pp 25-30).

The present name derives from J. B. S. Morritt, the squire of Rokeby, a house little more than a mile away. Morritt was a great traveller and his son, who was a connoisseur of pictures, owned the famous painting by Velasquez now in the National Gallery and known as the 'Rokeby Venus'. Morritt the elder was one of the closest friends of Sir Walter Scott whose journal of 1828 records:

He is now one of my oldest, and, I believe, one of my most

> sincere friends, a man unequalled in the mixture of sound good sense, high literary cultivation, and the kindest and sweetest temper that ever guided a human bosom.

Greta Bridge has always attracted artists and writers many of whom have used the Morritt Arms. John Sell Cotman, Thomas Girtin and J. M. W. Turner have all worked from the inn. It is said that Sir Walter Scott was staying here when he wrote the poem 'Rokeby'.

GUILDFORD, Surrey

The Angel in the High Street was probably a monastic foundation. A vaulted crypt beneath the building consists of three double bays of plain pointed rib-vaulting with two circular columns with plain bases, no capitals, and chamfered ribs. Almost exactly opposite, on the south side of the street, is a similar vault.[18] In the nineteenth century wall frescoes could be seen in the Angel crypt, one showing the flight into Egypt and the other the Crucifixion. Between the crypts from about 1345 the Fyshe Crosse stood in the centre of the High Street. It was erected by the White Friars and was surmounted by a flying angel carved in stone. It may be assumed that the inn derived its name and sign from this angel. By 1595 the cross had been removed to ease the movement of traffic. The order for its removal can still be seen in the *Guildford Court Book, 1586-1675.*

> . . . the fishe cross standinge neere the Aingell in the parishe of Saint Mary in Guldeford shal bee forthwith removed. And the place forr sellinge all kinde of freshe fishe shal bee at all tymes for ever hereafter kepte and used in the place where the same now standeth.

Stalls for the sale of fish were, in fact, erected in the centre of the High Street until 1820.

In the eighteenth century the inn became a noted coaching house on the Portsmouth Road and coaches left here for London as late as 1840. The words 'Posting House' and 'Livery Stables' remain as lettered signs on the façade above the old entrance to the courtyard.

HAMBLEDON, Hampshire

The Bat and Ball, originally The Hutt, is a small licensed house at a crossroads just over 2 miles east of Hambledon village at Broadhalfpenny Down.

This country inn will always be associated with the birth of the game of cricket as we know it today for the ground used by the Hambledon Club in the eighteenth century stretches out before it and is marked by a solid grey-granite stone inscribed:

> This stone marks the site of the Ground of the
> Hambledon Cricket Club circa 1750-1797

A carved panel shows two old-style bats and the original two wickets as used in the early game.

The Bat and Ball Inn has changed but the frontage is much as it was when the Hambledon Club was formed in 1850. So is the long-beamed bar. It naturally contains cricketiana but the bats used by the early players were taken some time ago to London and are now proud possessions of the Marylebone Cricket Club.

The famous period in the club's history was from 1770 when Richard Nyren was the secretary and also landlord of the inn which provided 'pavilion facilities'. On 17 June in that year the Hambledon Club defeated an All England team by an innings and 168 runs. The local farmers who watched the matches in those days drank punch at 6d a bottle, a potion 'that would make a cat speak', or maybe ale at 2d a pint 'that would put the soul of three butchers into one weaver'. Nyren's son, John was also a cricketer and in 1833 wrote *The Young Cricketer's Tutor.*

The games of cricket at Hambledon were often followed by musical evenings at the Bat and Ball. The sign of the inn commemorates Nyren and his players. On one side four cricketers are playing on a pitch with two wickets; on the other side is a portrait of John Nyren of Hambledon 1764-1837.

HATFIELD, Hertfordshire

The Eight Bells is a small Georgian alehouse with a tiled roof and large dormer windows, on the corner of Church Street. It is closely associated with Charles Dickens' novel *Oliver Twist* (1837-8). After Bill Sykes had brutally murdered Nancy he reached Hatfield with his dog at nine o'clock at night on his way to St Albans, and turning down 'the hill by the church of this quiet village and, plodding along the little street, crept into a small public house'. This was undoubtedly the Eight Bells at Hatfield. It was in the tap room that an antic fellow, half pedlar and half mountebank, after mentioning bloodstains, offered to remove the stain from Sykes' hat. Dickens knew Hatfield well. His diary records that he stayed in the town with Hablot Browne on 27 December 1838.

HAWKSHEAD, Lancashire

The Drunken Duck, once known as the Barngate Inn, is some distance from Hawkshead on the road to Ambleside (B5286). It is some 400 years old and changed its name in Victorian times. One day the landlady found six ducks, apparently dead, sprawled about on the ground before the front door. She picked them up, took them to her kitchen, and began to pluck them. Soon after she had finished they began to show signs of life. They had, in fact, been drinking beer which had leaked from a barrel in the yard. She was horrified and knitted little red jackets for them to wear until their feathers grew again. It is said that they recovered. From that day the inn has been known as the Drunken Duck.

HELMSLEY, Yorkshire

The Black Swan in the Market Place of this little stone-built town on the edge of the North Yorkshire moors dates from the sixteenth century (see p 53). It was a packhorse inn to which moorland farmers brought their wool. The three-storey stone frontage is late Georgian but many of the thick interior walls, oak ceiling timbers and fireplaces are original. The hall was panelled with Jacobean woodwork from the parish church when it was being rebuilt between 1849 and 1868. The Tudor stone doorway to the cellars was brought from Helmsley Castle.

The inn, known locally as the Mucky Duck, has always been

a focus for local life and was an important coaching and posting house. The annual rent dinners of the Duncombe estate are held at the Black Swan when the menu includes venison from the deer park. It is also a regular meeting place for the Sunnington Foxhounds.

In 1947 the inn was enlarged by the addition of a two-storey Georgian house with a fine staircase and in 1954 the old half-timbered and red-tiled vicarage next to the churchyard was added. Since then a new bedroom wing has been built at the rear.

HENLEY-ON-THAMES, Oxfordshire

The Angel is one of many old inns in Henley which was the crossing point on the River Thames for one of the main routes from London to the north-west. In fact there are three inns close to the bridge. On the south side (in Berkshire) is the **Carpenters Arms** with the date 1714 on the end wall. On the north side are the Red Lion and the Angel facing each other on opposite sides of the bridge.

The Angel may have been built on the site of an ancient hospice called the Hermitage, established with monies left for the purpose by John Longland, Bishop of Lincoln in the fourteenth century. The present building, which calls itself 'The Angel on the bridge', dates from the seventeenth century. This name no doubt derives from the fact that one of the cellars is built round a complete arch of an earlier Henley bridge. There are three storeys with bays, and a terrace overlooks the river. Since 1839 the Angel has catered for visitors to the Henley Royal Regatta.

The Red Lion dates from the seventeenth century and has a distinguished history as the main coaching inn of the town. It is said to have been built to accommodate the craftsmen and apprentices who built the near-by church of St Mary the Virgin. Charles I used the inn in 1632 and again, with Prince Rupert, in 1642 during the Civil War. There seems to be some evidence for this since a royal monogram dated 1632, found during building work in 1889, can still be seen in one of the rooms. In the early years of the eighteenth century the Duke of Marlborough kept a room at the inn for use on his journeys between London and Blenheim.

The present three storey brick building with its hipped roof is mainly Georgian.

William Shenstone, the poet, stayed at the inn in 1750 and is said to have scratched the following lines on a pane of glass:

> Whoe'er has travelled life's dull round,
> Where'er his stages may have been,
> May sigh to think how oft he found
> His warmest welcome at an inn.

Some say that these lines were to be seen on a window of the White Swan at Henly-in-Arden.

In 1776 Dr Johnson and James Boswell stayed at the Red Lion. Royalty used the inn on more than one occasion: George III made frequent visits, once with Queen Charlotte on 12 July 1788. When the Prince Regent visited the hotel he is said to have eaten fourteen mutton chops for which Mrs Dixon, the Red Lion's hostess, was famous.

After the Battle of Waterloo, the Duke of Wellington and General Blücher broke their journey at the Red Lion when they travelled to Oxford where the General was honoured with a Doctorate of Civil Law.

HERNE BAY, Kent

The Ship on the Central Parade, east of the pier, is a two-storey whitewashed building with weatherboarding on the second storey and an outside staircase to this floor which was once used for access to the old Coroner's Court Room where inquests were held. The room no longer exists for the interior has been completely re-designed and the wing on the street corner is now a private house for the inn tenants.

The inn dates back to the seventeenth century and a slipway opposite still runs from the road to the shore which was once used in 1666 to load vegetables on the boats for delivery in London after the Great Fire. It was here that smugglers also landed their goods, using the inn as their meeting place. One night Lieutenant Sydenham Snow, a young exciseman, heard that smugglers were due to land their cargo by the Ship and went with his men to arrest them. The smuggling gang proved to be so large that Snow's men fled and left him to cope single-handed. He was shot dead and, despite the fact that a trial was held at Bow Street, no one was convicted because no witnesses were willing to give evidence.

HIGHAM, Kent

The **Sir John Falstaff** (see p 54) on the London road is 3 miles west of Rochester and opposite to Gad's Hill Place, the home of Charles Dickens from 1857 and where he spent the last three years of his life and died in 1870. It is a seventeenth-century building of brick with a hipped, tiled roof with dormer windows. Later bay windows have been added to both storeys. The inn is said to have been built on the site where Sir John Falstaff caroused with Hal in Shakespeare's Henry IV.

In 1676 James Nevison, a highwayman nicknamed 'Swift Nicks' because of his skill with horses, robbed a traveller near the inn. Fearing that he had been recognised he rode to Gravesend, ferried across the river and then rode as fast as he could to York. Arriving on the same day, he changed and met the Lord Mayor of York on the bowling green. When he was later charged with the robbery at Gad's Hill he called on the Lord Mayor as witness that he was in Yorkshire on the day, claiming this as an alibi. This all happened long before Dick Turpin was born though it is said to be the origin of the story of Dick Turpin's ride to York as told by Harrison Ainsworth.

The Sir John Falstaff was often used by visitors who came to see Dickens at his Gad's Hill home.

HINDON, Wiltshire

The Lamb was an inn in the sixteenth century and the present stone building with its tiled roof became an important posting house in the eighteenth and nineteenth centuries.

W. H. Hudson stayed at the Lamb for several weeks in the spring and summer of 1909 and in *A Shepherd's Life* (1910) describes how he watched the birds around the inn and particularly those that nested close to his window:

. . . three pairs of birds—throstle, pied wagtail and flycatcher —breeding in the ivy covering the wall facing the village street. . . . There were at least twenty other pairs—sparrows, thrushes, blackbirds, dunnocks, wrens, starlings and swallows. Yet the inn was in the very centre of the village, and being an inn the most frequented and noisiest spot.

HINTON ADMIRAL, Hampshire

The Cat and Fiddle, about 3 miles north-east of Christchurch, is approached by the A35. It is an old thatched inn with lattice windows and walls mainly of whitewashed cob. The signs suggest that its name is derived from the nursery rhyme. One is in carved oak over the doorway, almost hidden by the deep thatch; the other is a painted post sign. Both show a cat with a fiddle and a cow jumping over the moon. However, the name is more likely to have been derived from that of Caterine la Fidèle, the name of the owner of the house in Domesday Book, or perhaps from Caton Fidèle, the sixteenth-century protestant who showed great devotion to her faith during the reign of Queen Mary. There was certainly a hospice for pilgrims here in the eleventh century, kept by the monks of Christchurch Priory.

In the eighteenth and nineteenth centuries the Cat and Fiddle became a rendezvous for the smugglers of Christchurch Bay and there is a secret hiding place in one of the old chimneys where contraband was hidden.

HITCHIN, Hertfordshire

The Sun in Sun Street probably existed early in the sixteenth century though the earliest recorded date is 1575. Late in the reign of Queen Elizabeth I the Michaelmas Court Leet and the Hitchen justices were meeting in an upper chamber of the inn and early in the seventeenth century the Archdeaconry Court, formerly held at an inn called The Angel, moved to the Sun which then became the leading hostelry in the town.

During the Civil War the inn was used by the Parliamentarians: here the freeholders of Hitchin signed their protestation to defend the High Court of Parliament. It became the headquarters for the 3,000 soldiers quartered in the town, and the

Council of War for Hertfordshire met at the inn and was visited there by leading Parliamentary figures including Cromwell, Hampden and Pym.

For many years after the Restoration the Sun was in the doldrums. It was boycotted by the restored nobility and gentry and apart from townsfolk and shopkeepers had little custom. Prosperity, however, returned with the coaching era. In 1741, John Shrimpton established the London–Hitchen and Bedford Coach which inned at the Sun, and other routes followed. In 1745 the local militia used it as a recruiting centre and meeting place when preparing to resist the advancing Jacobite forces. At about this time the Sun was largely rebuilt with the three-storey frontage of blue brick and the central carriageway seen today. An assembly room was added in 1770. Much of the earlier Elizabethan and Jacobean work still exists behind the Georgian façade.[19]

HOLFORD, Somerset

Alfoxton Park Hotel (formerly Alfoxden House) is a Queen Anne country mansion close to the A39, west of Bridgwater, and has been a hotel for a relatively short time. It lies well back from the road in some 50 acres of parkland and has two storeys, a central pediment and a roof with small dormer windows. There is a Tuscan porch approached by a drive. Its chief interest is in its association with William Wordsworth who once lived in the house for nearly a year.

William and Dorothy Wordsworth rented the property in 1797 for £23 a year, including taxes. Coleridge lived nearby at Nether Stowey and they met frequently and formed a close and creative friendship. Together they planned the *Lyrical Ballads* which were printed by Briggs & Cottle of Bristol and appeared in 1798. In a letter Coleridge referred to the house as

> . . . elegantly and completely furnished, with nine lodging rooms, three parlours and a hall, and in the most beautiful and romantic situation.

HULL, Yorkshire

Ye Olde White Harte is approached from Silver Street by a doorway and an alley. It was established in 1550 and is probably the oldest building in the city. The inn was restored in 1881 and it is now necessary to see the interior in order to sense its age. On the ground floor there is much panelling and two large brick fireplaces are inset with Delft tiles. A staircase, the woodwork rippled as the result of a fire, leads to the 'Plotting Parlour', a panelled room with fine early carving over the fireplace.

A panel in the bar tells the story of the events on St George's Day in 1642 when Charles I came to Hull.

> Whilst Sir John Hotham, the Governor of Hull, was giving a dinner party, he received an intimation from the King that His Majesty, who was then only four miles from the town, deigned to dine with him that day. The Governor, filled with surprise at the unexpected news, retired to his private room (since called The Plotting Room) and sent for Alderman Pelham, the M.P. for the Borough. It was then resolved to close the gates against the King and his followers and a message was despatched to His Majesty informing him of the decision which had been arrived at. The soldiers were called to arms, the bridge drawn up, the gates closed and the inhabitants confined to their houses. About 11 o'clock the King appeared at Beverley Gate but the Governor refused to allow him to enter the walls. The King then called upon the Major but that official fell upon his knees and swore that he could not assist, as the gates were guarded by soldiers. Whereupon the King after much strong conversation and proclaiming Hotham a traitor, withdrew to Beverley.

In the 1930s a secret room which contained human remains including a skull, was discovered in the roof of the inn. The skull is now preserved in the bar.

HUNGERFORD, Berkshire

The Bear, at one time the Black Bear, is an old inn on the A4 which was rebuilt in the eighteenth century and has had nineteenth-century additions, including a porch above which there is a painted wall sign. Henry VIII is said to have settled the original inn on Anne of Cleves and also on Catherine Howard.

The inn has associations with William of Orange but the accounts vary. One states that in 1688 when advancing to London to depose James he stayed at Littlecote House, just over 2 miles from Hungerford, and arranged to go to the Bear for a meal, only to find that it was a rendezvous for his enemies. The other version states that he reached Hungerford on 8 December 1688 and slept at the Bear. Here he received three emissaries led by Lord Halifax with a message from his father-in-law, James II.

HUNTINGDON

The George at the corner of High Street and George Street has a long history. It existed before Elizabeth I came to the throne and was sold in 1574 to Henry Cromwell who came from a local family of brewers and was probably the grandfather of Oliver Cromwell who was born nearby. Charles I is said to have made the inn his headquarters when he was at Huntingdon in 1645.

The main interest of the old inn lies in two seventeenth-century wings one of which has an open gallery overlooking the yard. This has a balustrade with late seventeenth-century turned balusters and panelled posts supporting the roof. It is supported on wooden posts in the form of columns with moulded capitals and bases. The gallery led to the bedrooms and the outer staircase leading to it is still well preserved (see p 54). The yard was once cobbled throughout its length.[20]

In the eighteenth century and until 1839 regular coaches on the old North Road used the inn on their way to and from London. The landlord in the 1830s was William Hennessy whose relative Thomas, who had for years been the respected driver of the famous Stamford 'Regent', came to Huntingdon to drive a two-horse omnibus between Huntingdon and Cambridge when railway competition had virtually killed the coaching trade.

In 1870 a fire swept the inn though happily the yard buildings escaped the flames. The present three-storey frontage of yellow brick with rusticated stucco on the ground floor was built after the fire. The view of the older red brick wing from the car park at the rear affords a striking contrast.

HURLEY, Berkshire

Ye Olde Bell in this Thames-side village is just over 4 miles east of Henley. It was founded as a hospice attached to the Benedictine Priory of St Mary (which became a cell of Westminster) in 1135. An underground passage between the inn and the priory building (now a private residence) is said to exist though it is no longer accessible.

The present two-storey building dates from the end of the sixteenth century. It is half-timbered but except at road level the wall timbers are covered with plasterwork. The upper storey, which overhangs slightly, carries several oriel windows, only one of which is original. This may be recognised by its moulded oak mullions and sill. The roof is broken by two gables one of which rises above a timbered porch.

HURSTBOURNE TARRANT, Hampshire

The George and Dragon on the Andover to Newbury road (A343) has probably been an inn since the eleventh century and parts of the present building are very old.[21] One of the second-storey rooms shows a half-timbered gable, now truncated, with vertical timbers which run through to the bar below. This central part of the house may well be sixteenth century or earlier. The deeds date back to 1735 and it was probably at this time that the property was enlarged and the Georgian frontage built. The old gable is obscured by a facing wall which carries a bracket sign (see p 71). At one time the inn was a posting house with stabling. An old letter dated 1756 sent from London to the village of Vernham Dean, higher up the Bourne valley, asks for a box to be sent by 'Mr. King's waggon of Newbury which will be at the George at Up-Husbon, Tuesday. The bookkeeper of ye waggon tells me he comes there Tuesdays and returns Fridays.' Hurstbourne Tarrant was known as Uphusband until well into the nineteenth century. The name was used by William Cobbett who knew the inn well for he often stayed with his friend Mr Blount who lived in a house across the road. 'Blount's cart horse, Tinker, could always be borrowed as a trace horse to help up the hill, and then unhitched at the top he would come back alone and put himself in the stable.' The George and Dragon no doubt supplied horses to help the coaches up the steep hill which in Cobbett's day was rough and difficult to climb with a load.

The two rectangular bays were probably added in Victorian times. One was probably used as a parcels office for there is a small kneehole desk built in under one window. Above the open fireplace in the bar is the original mail rack with pigeon holes where mail delivered by coach would await collection.

IPSWICH, Suffolk

The Great White Horse, at the junction of Northgate Street and Tavern Street, is a large rectangular Georgian building of three storeys built on the site of an old timbered inn which is known to have existed in 1518. The upper storeys are of weathered yellow brick, the ground floor is of rusticated stucco and carries a lettered sign which spans the frontage. Above the entrance is an effigy sign which Charles Dickens described in *Pickwick Papers* as '. . . a stone statue of some rampacious animal with flowing mane and tail, distantly resembling an insane cart horse . . .'

King George II stayed at the White Horse in 1736, receiving the dignitaries of Ipswich in an upstairs room despite the fact that he arrived after eleven o'clock at night. Most of the present building dates from the second half of the eighteenth century. In 1764 the Post Coaches left the inn every day at seven o'clock in the morning and arrived at the Black Bull in Bishopsgate, London at 5pm the same day.

Dickens first stayed at the Great White Horse in 1830 when he was sent to Ipswich to report a parliamentary election for the *Morning Chronicle*. Although his description of the hotel and its service in *Pickwick Papers* (1836-7) is disparaging, successive managements have found that it has had considerable publicity value. There is no doubt that Dickens needed to give the impression of an inn with 'labyrinths of uncarpeted passages' in order to lead up to the dramatic story of Mr

Pickwick's entry into the wrong bedroom where he encountered the 'middle-aged lady in yellow curl papers'.

Other notable visitors to the hotel have included King Louis VIII of France and, in 1800, Lord Nelson and Lady Hamilton.

ISLEWORTH, Middlesex

The London Apprentice is an old Georgian inn on the banks of the Thames, a three-storey brick building with a hipped roof and added bays. A terrace overlooks the river and there are two signs, a large lettered sign on the parapet, and a painted bracket sign on the front wall of a young apprentice in eighteenth-century costume. Apprentices from the London livery companies used to row up the river for a day's outing and drink ale in the old tavern and the inn has attracted boatmen ever since.

The name probably derives from the ballad of the *London Apprentice* who 'declared his matchless manhood and brave adventures done by him in Turkey and by what means he married the King's daughter of that same country'. His great feat was to have held a lion's heart in each hand as shown in the illustration from a seventeenth-century chapbook.

KENDAL, Westmorland

The Fleece in Highgate was established in 1654 and its name indicates the importance of Kendal as the southern gateway to the English Lake District when the roads were poor and fleeces from the fell sheep were brought by packhorse to this focal town. It is a three-storey building in black and white stucco. The upper storeys overhang and are supported by a row of pillars.

The Woolpack in Stricklandgate dates from about the same period and was one of the main centres for the Lakeland wool trade and a place where fell sheep farmers met the wool buyers. It also became an important coaching house and to serve this purpose was largely rebuilt c1781. The most striking feature is the enormous entrance to the old yard which occupies nearly half the width of the building. It was made to take the wide heavy waggons which replaced packhorses when the roads began to improve towards the end of the eighteenth century.

KESWICK-on-DERWENTWATER, Cumberland

The George, originally the George and Dragon, is the oldest inn in Keswick dating from Elizabethan times. At this period German miners prospected for minerals and dug ores of lead and silver in the local Goldscope workings. Their smelting house was at Keswick forge. Indentures were made between Queen Elizabeth and Thomas Thurland, Master of the Savoy, and Daniel Hechstatter of Augsburg under the Mines Royal Charter of 1561. The miners paid their dues to the queen's officers at the George and Dragon, the main centre of trade. It is said that unscrupulous traders also brought plumbago ore or 'wadd', stolen from the mines of Borrowdale, to be disposed of at the inn.

In 1715 the Earl of Derwentwater, on his last visit to Keswick, called at the inn for a tankard of ale before riding away to join the rebellion which ended with his death on the Tower Hill scaffold.

When George I came to the throne the George and Dragon became simply The George. In the nineteenth century it was a noted coaching inn used from time to time by Coleridge, Wordsworth and Southey. The late frontage is Georgian in style.

The Royal Oak also dates from Elizabethan times though the building today gives few clues to its origin. It was entirely

Page 89: *(right)* The White Hart Royal, Moreton-in-Marsh; *(below)* The George, Norton St Philip

Page 90: *(above)* Tudor wall paintings, The White Horse, Romsey; *(left)* the hallway of The Royal Hotel, Ross-on-Wye

rebuilt in the eighteenth century and became the headquarters of the packhorse trade and, as the roads improved, also became a posting house and a halting place for stage coaches.

John Teather, the landlord at the beginning of the nineteenth century, moved to Carlisle and set up a coaching business to operate on the route between Lancaster and Glasgow. In 1837 he was succeeded by his son but railway competition killed the trade and young Teather returned to Keswick where he, in turn, became landlord of the Royal Oak.

The hotel is proud of its literary associations. It was frequented by Coleridge, De Quincey, Shelley, Southey and Wordsworth, and it was here that Sir Walter Scott wrote his *Bridal of Triermain* (1813). Stevenson and Tennyson also stayed at the hotel.

A new wing was added to the hotel in 1930, designed by the architect, P. M. Hope.

KING'S LYNN, Norfolk

The Duke's Head in the Tuesday Market Place was built in 1685 on the site of an older inn called the Griffin, and was probably named after the Duke of York, who, as James II, came to the throne in that year. It was planned by a vintner, Sir John Turner, to meet a specific need. In those days the town had an important cloth trade and was a flourishing port where ships were built. The merchants who came to trade had to go to the Exchange (now the Customs House) which had been built in 1683. They needed accommodation in the town and Sir John provided it at the Duke's Head. The architect was Henry Bell, a local man and twice mayor of the town, who had already designed the Exchange. The hotel is an imposing three-storey building with a decorative cornice and broken pediment surmounted by a hipped roof with dormer windows (see p 71). Contemporary features include a fine stairway and panelled lounge. There have been considerable extensions.

No attempt was made in the early days to cater for coaching traffic but by the nineteenth century the Duke's Head had become the main terminus in the town; by 1850 the trade of the house had declined.

KIRKBY STEPHEN, Westmorland

The King's Arms, built at the end of the seventeenth century, is an old coaching inn in the Eden valley. It has three storeys and a Tuscan porch above which two Victorian bay windows have been built out, spoiling the line of the façade. The interior has a number of eighteenth-century features including Adam-style doors and a Georgian powder closet.

In the nineteenth century the King's Arms was an important stop for the mail coaches. In the winter of 1840 a coach left Sedburgh for Kirkby Stephen but when the driver made a call at the Cross Keys Inn at Cantley, the horses set off without him, carrying the passengers towards Kirkby Stephen. A male passenger tried to gain the driving seat and grasp the reins but fell off on the icy road. Later, he managed to secure a horse and followed the coach, only to find that the horses had drawn up outside the King's Arms. Miraculously, the passengers were safe and the coach continued to Spitals on Stainmore, driven by the passenger who had previously fallen from it.

Until recently the annual Luke Fair was held in the main Street in October and the King's Arms was thronged with sheep- and cattle-farmers. The sheep pens extended from the inn 'through Market Street, around Victoria Square, and up past the Methodist Church'.[22]

KIRKSTONE PASS, Westmorland

The Kirkstone Pass Inn, on the direct road from Ambleside via Ullswater to Penrith, is 1,468ft above sea level. It lies at a point where the Windermere and Ambleside roads converge before crossing the pass. The building is probably seventeenth century but did not become an inn until the nineteenth century when it was first known as The Traveller's Rest. It is a long, low, whitewashed house of two storeys, slate-roofed; the interior has stone floors and heavy timbering. The exterior is much as it was some 300 years ago but there have been changes inside to bring it up-to-date, inevitable with the metalling of the road over the pass, and the growth of motor traffic.

KNUTSFORD, Cheshire

The Royal George in King Street, formerly The George, dates from the fourteenth century and became a noted coaching inn in the eighteenth century, after rebuilding. John Byng describes it in his *Torrington Diaries* as it was in 1790:

> This inn is a very good one; the stabling likewise is good, and a wax candle was put into my bedroom . . . I had a diversity of cold viands for supper, as spitchcocked eel, cold fowl, cold lamb, tarts and custards. . . . In this inn are built assembly and tea rooms of spacious grandeur, where are held monthly assemblies; at which the maid bragged that none but gentility were admitted: but *on no account* any tradesmen.

Knutsford is Mrs Gaskell's *Cranford* (1853) where she was brought up by her aunt. This fine piece of descriptive writing reaches its climax when the chief characters 'were all assembled in the great parlour of the George'.

Anne Thackeray Ritchie, in a preface to the 1891 edition of *Cranford*, described her own visit to the inn:

> As we entered the Royal George Hotel out of the dark street, we came upon a delightful broadside of shining oak staircase and panelled wainscote; old oak settles and cupboards stood upon the landings. On the wall hung pictures, one was of Lord Beaconsfield, one was a fine print of George IV . . . There were Chippendale cabinets, old bits of china, and above all there were the beautiful oak bannisters to admire.

The inn was visited by Princess Victoria on her way to Chatsworth, by Louis Napoleon (later Napoleon III), and by Sir Walter Scott when travelling to Abbotsford.

The Angel in King Street, built in the Queen Anne style, was also a coaching inn in the eighteenth century and is also mentioned in *Cranford*. It derives its name from the mermaid in the ancient coat of arms of the Mere family of Mere, Cheshire. The inn seems to have been concerned more with the business life of Knutsford than was the George. In the 1780s auctions were held at which timber was sold to shipbuilders and the Angel was the inn where horses had to be entered for the local races.

LAVENHAM, Suffolk

The Swan, with road frontages in High Street and Water Street, dates from Tudor times when Lavenham already had a prosperous weaving industry and cloth was exported to Europe by merchants who had grown rich on the proceeds. They built a Guildhall, a Wool Hall and many fine houses. Four of these fifteenth-century houses, each one half-timbered with an oversailing upper storey and steep gables, were united in the seventeenth century as the Swan (see p 72). Extensive stabling was provided for the many packhorses which brought wool and cloth from the nearby villages such as Lindsey and Kersey which were noted weaving centres. The plasterwork on the house which forms the corner of Water Street has a Tudor rose and a fleur-de-lys surmounted by a mitre, the emblem of Bishop Blaize, patron saint of wool combers.

The hostelry flourished and in 1667 John Girling, the innkeeper, issued his own trade tokens. In the eighteenth century coaching traffc became important and a carriageway led into the courtyard. The 'Lavenham Machine' left the Swan three days a week for the Spread Eagle in Gracechurch Street, London. By 1830 the posting trade had become more important.

Considerable changes were made in the eighteenth and nineteenth centuries. Much of the timbering was covered with plasterwork, open fireplaces were closed and eventually the carriageway was bricked up and the stables made into a dining room. Happily, a change of ownership in 1933 led to a major restoration. Timbering was exposed, fireplaces were opened up, and the old carriageway became the entrance hall. In 1962 the fifteenth-century Wool Hall at the corner of Water Street and Lady Street was acquired and incorporated. The architect, James Hopwood, created lounges where the old Courtyard had been and knitted old and new together in harmony by building a large dining hall in Tudor style, using Suffolk craftsmen to shape the timbers.

During World War II, when East Anglia was studded with British and American air bases, many members of Bomber and Fighter Command and the US Army Air Corps frequented the Swan at Lavenham. They sometimes wrote their names on the smoke room walls before leaving on important missions and these signatures are still preserved. So is the half gallon glass boot they used for competitive drinking. The record ' swig ' is said to have taken a mere 22 seconds!

LECHLADE-ON-THAMES, Gloucestershire

The Trout is on the Faringdon Road, less than a mile out of Lechlade, and stands by St John's Bridge over the Thames, close to its confluence with the River Leach. It is a typical stone-built Cotswold house with timbered ceilings and has a long history. A hospice or almshouse attached to a priory of the Black Monks was established on the site in 1472 by Peter Fitzherbert. In the reign of Edward IV the hospice became an inn, Ye Sygne of St John Baptist Head. In 1704 it was renamed The Trout Inn.

Not surprisingly it is a fisherman's inn and has 3 miles of water under fishing rights which originally were granted by King John to the medieval priors.

LEDBURY, Herefordshire

The Feathers in the High Street is one of a number of Elizabethan buildings in the town. It was built in 1560, is heavily timbered with close-set uprights, and has five gables. Although the main building dates from the sixteenth century, an additional storey was added later and a new wing was built in the seventeenth century. For many years the timbers were covered with plaster which was only removed in the nineteenth century. An assembly room at the back was built on pillars over the courtyard. The coaching trade began in about 1770 and coaches were still calling at the inn a hundred years later.

The Talbot in New Street carries the date 1596 which derives from a panelled room inside. The gabled frontage, which is timbered with close-set uprights and horizontal bracing, dates from the seventeenth century. A large canted bay window above the entrance breaks the line of the building and is later still. The interior has an oak-panelled room with a fine Jacobean mantelpiece. This room is still much as it was when it was the scene of a clash between Prince Rupert's followers and supporters of Cromwell after the Battle of Ledbury. Two bullet holes in the panelling are said to have been made on this occasion.

In the eighteenth century the Talbot became a coaching house.

LEWES, Sussex

The White Hart in the High Street gives little appearance of age. The frontage was built in the nineteenth century, but behind this are many features which date back to the sixteenth century when it was the home of the Pelham family. At this period the wine cellars were used as a dungeon during the persecution of the Protestants. Many of the beams used in the old building came from shipbuilders' yards on the River Ouse.

The Pelhams were elevated to the peerage early in the eighteenth century and, as the Dukes of Newcastle, moved across the street to Newcastle House and their old property became an inn c1717. The first landlord of the White Hart was Richard Verral who made it into a coaching establishment and built up such a reputation for good food that many local banquets were held in the inn, including election parties. In 1737 he died and was succeeded by his fifth son, William Verral, who not only kept up the reputation for good food but also produced a book, *The Compleat System of Cookerie.*

In 1761 Tom Paine, who frequently came to the White Hart to meet his friends and to play bowls, founded a political discussion club in the inn which later came to be known as the Headstrong Club because of the radical views expressed by its members. Tom Paine later described the White Hart as 'the cradle of American Independence'.

On 8 January 1820 William Cobbett stopped at the inn with a friend, Mr Brazier. His diary records:

> We put up at the White Hart, took another chaise and went round and saw the farms through the windows of the chaise. Came back to the White Hart after being absent only about an hour and a half, got our dinner, and got back to Worth before it was dark.

On 1 October 1929 the British Foreign Secretary, Arthur Henderson, and the envoy of the Soviet Republic, M. Dorgalevsky, met in the White Hart to discuss the relations between the two countries. An agreement was reached and diplomatic relations were resumed. The Foreign Secretary was criticised for this 'White Hart Treaty' as it was called and Mr Stanley Baldwin accused him of surrendering to Russian demands 'at a hotel where bitter beer is sold and where cricketers are wont to resort'. 'I think the Foreign Secretary was playing a straight bat very carefully,' he went on, 'but after lunching with the Soviet representative he collapsed'.

South Street, Lewes becomes the Eastbourne Road (A27) and on the left a short distance from the town stands a small public house called **The Snowdrop Inn** at the foot of a steep chalk hill. The origin of the name is surprising and has nothing to do with the spring flower. On the eve of Christmas 1836, when the snow was deep on the ground, a storm brought down a mass of snow from the hill above and buried the inhabitants of a group of cottages below. Eight people died and there is a tablet to them in Malling Church. The Snowdrop Inn now marks the site of the disaster.

LICHFIELD, Staffordshire

The George in Bird Street carries a plaque with this information:

> George Farquhar (1677-1707) lived in the inn on this site whilst as a lieutenant of Grenadiers in 1705 he was recruiting troops in Lichfield. The inn he immortalised in his comedy *The Beaux Stratagem*.

No doubt his experiences whilst recruiting were well used in his other late play *The Recruiting Officer* (1706). *The Beaux Stratagem* was published in 1707, the year in which he died.

The Swan, also in Bird Street, is an old coaching inn. It dates back to the seventeenth century for the Lansdown Manuscripts in the British Museum describe a visit of three soldiers, a captain, lieutenant and cornet of horse to Lichfield in 1634:

> Thither were we quickly brought to the Lily White Swan in that sweet little City, and no sooner were we lighted than the Cathedral knell called us away to prayers.

The Swan Inn is mentioned several times by Dr Johnson in his diaries.

LINCOLN

The Green Dragon (or **Great Garrett)**, close to Pelham Bridge, probably belonged in the fourteenth century to St Catherine's Priory. In the sixteenth century it was a merchant's house. In 1567 the Mayor, Aldermen and Common Council of the City of Lincoln bought the property from Thomas Grantham. The first tenant was Peter Gollande, a weaver, and when he died in 1587, the lease passed to Hugh Moxon who is thought to have added the second or garret floor. At all events, the next tenant, Thomas Johnston, a baker, referred to the premises in 1624 as Great Garrett. In 1702 Alderman Benjamin Harris took over from the Johnson family, and within a few years the property, or part of it, became an inn. Thomas Sympson, the Lincoln antiquary who died in 1750, refers in his history of the city to 'the Green Dragon Ale House'. However, this was not the original Great Garrett but probably an adjoining property. A Victorian house on the site was pulled down in 1955 when the Pelham Bridge was built and the license was transferred to the Great Garrett which was restored in 1956-7 when the fine sixteenth-century timber frame was exposed.

The Cardinal's Hat, though no longer an inn, should nevertheless be seen by anyone interested in old timbered buildings. It dates from the late fifteenth century and was well restored in 1952-3. The ground floor is occupied by a building society. A Lincoln Civic Trust plaque explains that the name was probably given in compliment to Cardinal Wolsey who was Bishop of Lincoln, 1514-15.

LIPHOOK, Hampshire

The Royal Anchor in the Square is on the site of an earlier inn. Some say that it was originally a royal hunting lodge used by Edward II in 1310; others that it dates from 1415. Samuel Pepys certainly stayed at the inn with his wife in 1668 and the present building would appear to date from about this period. It has two storeys and rooms on the second floor have dormer windows in the hipped roof. Below the roof-line there is an egg-and-dart frieze.

The Anchor was a famous posting and coaching house on the Portsmouth road between Hindhead and Petersfield and many famous people have stayed there. In 1815 the Prince Regent arrived from London and lunched at the Anchor with the Duke of Wellington and his Russian ally, Marshal Blucher, after the victory at Waterloo. The dinner service used on this occasion is still on display. The inn was also used by Admiral Lord Nelson on his journey to Portsmouth before Trafalgar. 'He drank tea by candlelight at the Anchor, Liphook'[23] and arrived in Portsmouth at 6am on 14 September 1805.

Prisoners of war from Portsmouth Docks were chained in the Anchor's cellars overnight on their journey to prison and some say that the inn was used by smugglers and that a tunnel which connects the hotel with a near-by house was used when they wished to evade the excise officers.

Queen Victoria visited the Anchor as a girl with her mother the Duchess of Kent.

LONDON

The Black Friars (174 Victoria Street, Blackfriars, EC4) is a unique public house close to the railway bridge which crosses Queen Victoria Street, and also to Blackfriars Bridge. It is said to have been built on the site of an old Dominican priory. The style is pure *art nouveau*. The main bar has metal murals showing monks catching fish ('Tomorrow will be Friday'), collecting fruit ('Saturday Afternoon') and singing ('Carols'). The metal lampbrackets and the clock all show *art nouveau* designs with flowing lines, and the window has a stained glass panel of a scene with monks.

The room beyond the main bar is of coloured marble with a mosaic ceiling and the walls are decorated with bronzes and murals by Henry Poole RA, each with its 'turn of the century' motto—'Don't Advertise it'; 'Tell a Gossip'; 'Finery is foolery';

'Haste is Slow'; 'Industry is All'; 'A Good Thing is soon Snatched up'; 'Seize Occasion'; 'Wisdom is Rare'; and 'Silence is Golden'. Here the metal light fitments are in the form of monks using yokes to carry buckets.

The Old Bull and Bush (North End Way, Hampstead NW3) was built in 1645 as a farmhouse on the edge of Hampstead Heath. For some years it was the home of William Hogarth who planted a bower of yews. The 'Bush' in the name is said to have been derived from the yews, the 'Bull' from the farmhouse, though it would seem more likely that the 'bush' was added as the traditional sign for an inn.

In the days when William Pitt, 1st Earl of Chatham, lived at North End House which was put at his disposal by Charles Dingley, Hampstead village became a fashionable area, and the Bull and Bush was used by such notable figures as Thomas Gainsborough, David Garrick, Sir Joshua Reynolds and Laurence Sterne. Sometimes they would meet there for breakfast. 'Faith' exclaimed Gainsborough on one such occasion as he poured the new milk into his breakfast cup, 'there is cream upon't—and what a tablecloth! Damask—Dutch damask by the Lord.'

In the nineteenth century it was still popular with writers and artists—Charles Lamb, Charles Dickens, Charles Keene and George du Maurier. Then came the music hall song—'Down at the Old Bull and Bush' made famous by Florrie Forde which made it known throughout the country in Edwardian days. Since then it has been largely reconstructed and today shows little sign of age.

Ye Olde Cheshire Cheese (Wine Office Court, Fleet Street, EC4) is approached through an archway on the north side of Fleet Street. The building dates from 1667 and is on the site of an earlier inn destroyed in the Great Fire of London. One hundred years later it must have been well known to Dr Samuel Johnson who lived just round the corner. The cellars of the original tavern are still there and much of the atmosphere of Dr Johnson's day remains, at least on the ground floor. The bar to the right of the entrance has old panelled walls and ceiling, a dog grate, scrubbed tables and a sawdust-covered floor. The window seat is said to have been used by Johnson and also by Goldsmith who lodged in Wine Office Court. Above the fireplace is a painting of William Simpson, a waiter in the Chop House in 1829. The Chop House itself, to the left of the entrance, is similarly furnished.

Outside the tavern is a summary of its associations:

> 'Sir' said Dr. Johnson 'if you wish to have a just notion of the magnitude of this great City you must not be satisfied with seeing its streets and squares but must survey the innumerable little lanes and courts.'
>
> This lane takes its name from the Excise Office which was here up to 1665. Voltaire came, and, says tradition, Congreve and Pope. Dr. Johnson lived in Gough Square (end of the Court on the left) and finished his great dictionary there in 1775. Oliver Goldsmith lived at No. 6 where he partly wrote *The Vicar of Wakefield* and Johnson saved him from eviction by selling the book for him. Here came Johnson's friends—Reynolds, Gibbon, Garrick, Dr. Burney, Boswell and others of the circle. In the nineteenth century came Carlyle, Macauley, Tennyson, Dickens (who mentions the Court in *A Tale of Two Cities*), Forster, Hood, Thackeray, Cruikshank, Leech and Wilkie Collins. More recently came Mark Twain, Theodore Roosevelt, Conan Doyle, Beerbohm, Chesterton, Dowson, Le Gallienne, Symons, Yeats and a host of others in search of Dr. Johnson and 'The Cheese'.

The Cheshire Cheese is noted for its pies and puddings, particularly for 'Ye Pudding', weighing over half a hundredweight, and made to an old recipe with beefsteak, kidneys, mushrooms, etc, which is cut on the first Monday in October. The ceremony has been performed by many noted visitors including Stanley Baldwin, Conan Doyle, Jack Dempsey and Dean Inge.

The City Barge (27 Strand-on-the-Green, Chiswick, W4) lies on the north side of the Thames east of Kew Bridge which was first built to span the river in 1788. It will be found among a row of houses strung along the riverside towpath. It is a fifteenth-century tavern of bars with low timbered ceilings and old wooden settles. In the corner of one bar is a late eighteenth-century Parliament clock (1797) recalling the days when there was a tax on clocks and watches so that people who wished to avoid paying it had to rely on clocks in public places.

Outside the City Barge hangs a splendid sign showing the ceremonial craft carrying civic dignitaries down the river. The Corporation Barge of the City of London was once moored at Strand-on-the-Green and when the Lord Mayor and Aldermen used it, it was here they embarked. The barge was then towed by horses as far as Hampton Court. It was built in 1816 and named *Maria Wood*, after the daughter of Sir Mathew Wood. The length was 136ft and it was repaired in 1851 and sold in 1859.

There were earlier official barges. The eighteenth-century barge was stationed at Fulham Bridge and was used for collecting tolls. This was known as the Navigation Barge. A letter of 1780[24] refers to:

> . . . the Navigation Barge with my Lord and Lady Mayoress going the boundaries of the river, which drew people of all ranks down to the waterside. As I believe they call it the swan-hopping season, all the gardens next the river are lined with ladies and gentlemen to see the show and hear the music which brings down all the belles to show off.

Ye Olde Cock Tavern (22 Fleet Street, EC4) on the south side of Fleet Street has a relatively recent 'Tudor' façade and describes itself as 'famous for food since 1549'. It was originally the Cock and Bottle at No 201 on the north side of the street and was certainly a flourishing tavern in the seventeenth century when it issued trade tokens. It closed in 1665 because of the plague, but by 1668 it had reopened for Samuel Pepys informs us that he went 'by water to the Temple and then to the Cock alehouse and drank and eat a lobster, and sang, and mighty merry'. Samuel Johnson often dined there: the chair he used at the old Cock tavern is now preserved in his house in Gough Square.

Two hundred years later the inn was frequented by Alfred Tennyson who often dined there with Edward FitzGerald. It was the subject of his poem 'Will Waterproof's lyrical Monologue made at the Cock' which begins:

O Plump head-waiter at the Cock,
To which I most resort,
How goes the time? 'Tis five o'clock.
Go fetch a pint of port:
But let it not be such as that
You set before chance comers,
But such whose father grape grew fat
On Lusitanian summers.

In 1887 the Cock Tavern moved across the street and a few of the furnishings were taken to the new premises, among them a James I chimneypiece. There is also a wooden panel said to have been carved by Grinling Gibbons which may have been an earlier inn sign. These relics are now in the Dickens Room on the first floor.

In the days of Samuel Pepys the house was noted for its rum punch. In 1952 many distinguished citizens of London, headed by the Lord Mayor, Sir Rupert de la Bere, MP, 'acclaimed with good fellowship a truly noble Jamaican Rum Punch, the same being concocted from the receipt devised in years before at this tavern for consumption by one Samuel Pepys of London, Gentleman and Good Citizen'.

The Dove (19 Upper Mall, Hammersmith, W6), an unspoiled tavern beside the Thames at Hammersmith Pier, is a two-storey building with tiled roof and stuccoed walls, probably part of two sixteenth-century buildings at one time used as a single house. In the second quarter of the eighteenth century they were separated. No 17 Upper Mall was called The Seasons and No 19 The Dove. It is thought that James Thomson, the poet (who wrote the words for 'Rule Britannia'), occupied a room in the upper storey of No 17 when he came to London in 1725 and that he may have completed his poem 'Winter' here. There are certainly lines in the poem which may have been inspired when watching ice form on the Thames: '. . . Seized from shore to shore, the whole imprisoned river grows below'. 'Winter' was the first of four poems brought together in 1730 as *The Seasons*.

Later, part of No 17 was set aside as a smoking room for

the Duke of Sussex, one of Queen Victoria's uncles, where he could enjoy his 'social tube'.

Behind the tavern there is an iron balcony at first floor level beneath which a vine grows freely under a glass roof. In front of this extends a terrace with fine views of the river. Here J. M. W. Turner came to paint scenes of the Thames.

Many people from all walks of life still frequent the Dove. An illuminated testimonial over the brick fireplace of the bar carries the names (too many to list) of actors and actresses, authors and journalists, cricketers, painters and musicians anxious to express their appreciation of its atmosphere and hospitality.

The painted sign of the inn shows parting clouds which reveal a dove carrying a branch to the ark.

Close to the Dove is Kelmscott House where George Macdonald, the novelist, lived from 1867-77 and William Morris, craftsman and socialist, from 1878-96.

The Flask Tavern (77 Highgate West Hill, N6) is on the site of a fifteenth-century tavern but the present three-storey building in two shades of red brick was actually built in 1767 although it bears the date 1663. Hampstead Heath lies between the Flask Tavern and Flask Lane where the chalybeate springs were discovered in the eighteenth century which made Hampstead a spa. The water could be bought in flasks either at the springs or at the tavern—hence its name.

The Flask, together with the other Highgate taverns, used to observe an ancient ceremony:

It's a custom at Highgate that all who go through,
Must be sworn on the horns, sir; and so, sir, must you.
Bring me the horns, shut the door; now, sir, take off your hat,
When you come here again, don't forget to mind that.

The ceremony was usually carried out by the landlord dressed in a black gown and wearing a mask. One of his staff would carry the horns of an ox fixed to a pole. The traveller was then expected to remove his hat, and at the appropriate point in the ceremony to kiss the horns although if ladies were present he was allowed to kiss the girl of his choice instead. H. E.

Popham puts forward one theory to account for the custom:[25]

> . . . the Highgate inns were the resort of graziers bringing cattle from the Midlands to Smithfield . . . these men, wishful of securing accommodation for themselves, formed a kind of fraternity and made it imperative for all who desired to join them to take an oath and kiss the horns—in all probability originally an ox itself.

The Flask Tavern was much favoured by artists including, in their day, William Hogarth, George Morland and George Cruikshank.

The George (Borough High Street, Southwark, SE1), close to London Bridge Station, is the only galleried inn to have survived in London. The road which runs south-west from the bridge has always taken a considerable flow of traffic. This was the road used by pilgrims on their way to Canterbury and by travellers to the countries of Europe. In the sixteenth century it had a string of inns. John Stow, describing the approach to London Bridge, wrote of:

> . . . many fair inns for the receipt of travellers, by these signs. The Spurre, Christopher, Bell, Queene's Head, Tabarde, George, Harte, King's Head . . .

Plays were often staged in the yards of these inns and Shakespeare is said to have acted at the George. The inns escaped in the Great Fire of 1666 but ten years later a fire started in an oil shop early one morning and spread along the street destroying houses and hostelries. The George was rebuilt on its former site. Until the eighteenth century London Bridge remained the only crossing of the Thames and inns were becoming increasingly important on the main coaching routes. Several of these converged on London Bridge and fanned out on the southern side to Rochester, Maidstone, Tonbridge and Reigate. The coaches all passed the George which became an important coaching centre.

In the nineteenth century the George Inn was taken over by the Great Northern Railway Company when coach traffic was dwindling. In 1889 it was partially rebuilt and now only one wing of the earlier structure remains. In this wing the gallery leading to the bedrooms may still be seen. Charles Dickens mentions the inn in *Little Dorrit* (1856-7). Tip, her brother, wrote letters to Clennane from the inn. In 1937 the George was given to the National Trust.

Jack Straw's Castle (Spaniards Road, Hampstead, NW3), once known as The Castle, is close to White Stone Pond, the highest point in London (440ft). It has existed for over 200 years for Samuel Richardson mentions it in *Clarissa* (1747-8). At one time the inn appears to have been run by a Mrs Jack Straw, and must surely have gained its present name during her occupation and not, as has sometimes been suggested, from Jack Straw, one of the leaders of the peasant revolt in 1381.

In the nineteenth century there were extensive tea gardens and there is still a fenced-in brick-paved beer garden at the rear. The inn is mentioned in Washington Irving's *Tales of a Traveller* (1824) and later it was frequented by Dickens, Thackeray, George du Maurier and Lord Leighton. Dickens is said to have persuaded his biographer, John Forster, to join him on one of his trips to Hampstead with these words: 'I know a good 'ouse where we can have a red-hot chop for dinner and a glass of wine'. This was Jack Straw's Castle which now, inevitably, has a Dickens room. Most of the building is modern, covered with weatherboards and decorated with timber cornices, battlements and a turret. It has pseudo-gothic sash windows and wood-panelled rooms. The rebuilding which took place between 1961 and 1964 under the direction of Raymond Erith, RA, FRIBA, gained a Civic Trust commendation.

The Mitre (Ely Court, Ely Place, EC1) was originally built by Bishop Goodrich in 1546 on part of the garden of the London Palace of the Bishops of Ely. The present building, however, is eighteenth century but built into the façade is a carved and painted stone mitre which appears to be earlier. In a corner of the saloon bar there is part of a cherry tree around which Queen Elizabeth is said to have danced the maypole. In fact this tree marked the boundary between the bishop's garden and the land leased to Sir Christopher Hatton by Bishop Cox in Elizabeth's reign. The Mitre is built on Cambridgeshire land

Page 107: The Mermaid, Rye

Page 108: *(above)* The White Hart, Salisbury, *(left)* panel of the Chevy Chase sideboard, The Grosvenor Shaftesbury

and keeps Cambridgeshire hours. The keeping of law and order in Ely Place and Ely Court is the responsibility of beadles. These sanctuary rights are jealously preserved and no policeman enters this territory. At night the lodge gates are locked.

The Mitre is not easy to find: leave Holborn Circus by way of Hatton Garden and a doorway 50yd along on the right leads into Ely Court and to the inn.

The Nag's Head (Covent Garden, WC2) is on the corner formed by Floral Street and James Street, directly opposite Covent Garden Market and very close to the Royal Opera House and the Theatre Royal, Drury Lane. Its main interest has always been in the clientele. For years it has had a special licence to open at 6.30am for the fruit salesmen who use it throughout the day. Later, journalists from Long Acre, men from the Bow Street courts, local businessmen, actors and singers during rehearsal breaks, and evening theatregoers use its bar and first floor restaurant. The walls of the saloon bar and the staircase are covered with original playbills, caricatures by Cruikshank and others, and portrait engravings of playwrights and actors. There is one of Richard Brinsley Sheridan, for example, who for thirty years owned the Theatre Royal where three of his most famous plays were produced.

On the first floor there is a collection of theatrical designs by Cecil Beaton, Oliver Messel and Tanya Moiseiwitsch.

Nell of Old Drury (Catherine Street, Covent Garden, WC2) is opposite the Theatre Royal which was opened in 1660. It probably dates from this period and may be even older. In its early days it was known as the Lamb and it is said that a passageway was made between the inn and the theatre which could be used by the theatre staff. Charles II is said to have used this passage instead of crossing the road when he wished to meet Nell Gwynn at the Lamb. Sheridan who owned the theatre from 1776 may have had an interest in the Lamb. His new theatre was opened in 1794 and prospered until it was destroyed by fire in 1809, ending Sheridan's reign as owner and manager.

In the 1820s the name of the inn was changed to the Sir John Falstaff and in the 1960s to the Nell of Old Drury. The earlier frontage is gone. The present mahogany door and window frames are set back so that the first floor of the building overhangs the pavement.

The Prospect of Whitby (Wapping Wall, E1) was built on its Thames-side site at Shadwell in 1520 when it was known as Devil's Tavern. It was later named The Prospect of Whitby after a Yorkshire sailing vessel from Whitby called *The Prospect* which used to moor at Wapping Wall. It has always been a tavern for sailors and watermen. The building appears to stand on stilts and smugglers are said to have passed up tobacco through trap doors from their boats below the balcony.

Samuel Pepys visited the tavern in the days when the sport of knuckle-fighting was in vogue, and cock-fighting was certainly carried on in those days. The execution dock for pirates was nearby and Judge Jeffreys is said to have watched the proceedings from the balcony of the tavern which overhangs Pelican Stairs. He is said to have later hidden at the tavern in the guise of a common sailor when trying to flee the country. He was certainly caught at Wapping before being sent to the Tower to save him from the mobs.

In the nineteenth century the tavern was a favourite haunt of J. M. W. Turner the artist, and Charles Dickens found it a useful place to study some of the tougher characters of East London.

The Spaniards Inn (Spaniards Road, Hampstead, NW3) dates from 1630 or even earlier and was built on the sandy soil of Hampstead Heath where the old lodge entrance to the Bishop of London's rural park once stood. The origin of the name is uncertain. Some say that the first landlord was a Spaniard; others that the Spanish Ambassador to James I lived in a house on the site.

The inn has had some notable landlords, among them Giles Thomas who, in 1780, discovered that Kenwood House in the near-by parkland was in danger from Gordon rioters who, in an anti-popery demonstration, had just burned down Lord Mansfield's house. Thomas managed to keep them occupied at the Spaniards while the ostler alerted a contingent of the Horse Guards.

The Spaniards was used by Keats and Coleridge when they lived nearby and also by Byron, Shelley and Sir Joshua Reynolds. Early in May 1819 Joseph Severn went to the Spaniards with a party of friends which included John Keats. During the evening Keats was found to be missing and was later discovered by Severn lying beneath some trees listening to the song of the nightingales. A few days later in Wentworth Place he wrote his famous 'Ode to a Nightingale'.

Dickens knew the Spaniards well; he used the inn in *Pickwick Papers* (1836-7). Mrs Bardell and her friends, determined to have a day out, took the Hampstead coach to the Spaniards Tea Gardens where she was arrested by the agents of Dodson and Fogg. A garden area is still available for the use of customers.

The Tom Cribb (24 Panton Street, Haymarket, SW1) was called the Union Arms when, through the generosity of his sporting friends Tom Cribb became the landlord in 1811 after his retirement as 'Champion Boxer of all England'. Although the present building with its façade of brown glazed tiles is relatively modern, Tom Cribb is remembered in the name and the interior wall decoration where old prints and bills recall his fighting career for he was one of the greatest boxers of all time. His first three successful fights were against Jim Maddox, Tom Black and Ikey Pigg. He defeated Jem Belcher in 1809 in thirty-one rounds and Tom Molyneaux the negro boxer, in 1810 in thirty rounds and again in 1811 in eight rounds.

When Tom Cribb took the Union Arms he established what was known as 'Tom Cribb's Parlour' which attracted sportsmen, artists, actors and men of letters. John Emery, the actor and artist, Lord Byron, William Hazlitt, Thomas Moore and John Reeves, a lawyer at the Board of Trade, were all 'regulars'. Byron wrote in his diary in 1812:

> Midnight—just returned from dinner with Jackson (The Emperor of Pugilism), and another of the select, at Cribb's . . . We had Cribb up after dinner: very facetious though somewhat prolix. He don't like his situation ; wants to fight again ; pray Pollux (or Castor, if he was the Miller) he may. Tom . . .

is now only thirty three. A great man. Tom is an old friend of mine: I have seen some of his best battles in my nonage. He is now a publican and, I fear, a sinner.

In 1837 Renton Nicholson produced these lines about the inn:

> At the Union Arms in Panton Street,
> Lives Tom of vast renown;
> A better man, or jollier dog,
> Is nowhere in our town.
>
> Your grog, old boy, is excellent
> And nowhere do we meet,
> More social fun and merriment
> Than at yours, in Panton Street.

The Trafalgar Tavern (Park Road, Greenwich) is on a site once occupied by an alehouse known as the Old George Inn, The Trafalgar Tavern was built in 1837 to a design by John Kay, the surveyor of Greenwich Hospital. Charles Dickens knew the Trafalgar Tavern well: it was here that he met Douglas Jerrold, the author and dramatist, for the last time and he mentions the inn in *Our Mutual Friend* (1864-5).

In the 1850s the Trafalgar Hotel was famous for serving thirty fish courses. They were described by a party of Frenchmen from Paris:[26]

> Such an exhibition of new dishes, unknown and unrecognisable, was as interesting to us as any museum. As with Aesop's tongues, fish is disguised in a variety of ways. Turbot, salmon, sole, sturgeon are served with incendiary sauces that stagger and parch one. These peppery concoctions left me unmoved if not cold—but a *friture* of whitebait really is a dish to set before a king. As these microscopic gudgeons are only to be found in the Thames it was a novelty for us and one we are not likely to forget.

In 1883 the Liberals under Gladstone had their last dinner in the Trafalgar Tavern. No doubt there were whitebait on the menu for these little fish are traditionally served in Greenwich though they are no longer taken from the Thames.

In 1908 the tavern closed and was used for various purposes for some years until its relatively recent restoration as an inn.

The Yorkshire Stingo (Marylebone Road, NW1), named after a strong malt liquor, was a great social centre in the nineteenth century. It had tea gardens and a bowling green and on Sundays sixpence was charged for admission. Plays were performed on a stage in the garden but such tavern theatres were not allowed to play Shakespeare; 'high class' drama was restricted to the West End.

In 1829 George Shillibeer introduced the first London omnibus which started from The Yorkshire Stingo and ran to the Bank for a shilling (5p) fare for which passengers were also given a newspaper.

LONG MELFORD, Suffolk

The Bull on the A134, 3 miles north of Sudbury, was built c1450 when the town had a flourishing woollen trade manned mainly by immigrant Flemish weavers. It started as the house of a wealthy cloth merchant with workshops on the premises and became an inn c1570. It is a two-storey, half-timbered building with close-set uprights and tall brick chimneys (see p 72). The timbered frontage was hidden behind brickwork from early Victorian times and was only uncovered in 1935. The carved uprights and spandrels of the entrance doorway are probably seventeenth century. Inside there are many carved and moulded beams, a weaver's gallery and a sixteenth-century brickwork hearth. On one of the massive uprights near the door of the lounge is the carved figure of a 'wodewose' or wild-man.

In July 1648, during the Civil War, a well-to-do Melford yeoman, Richard Evered, was attacked and killed in the entrance hall of the inn. His body was buried in the nearby churchyard. His assailant, Roger Greene, was convicted of murder and executed.[27]

In coaching days the Bull was the chief posting house of the town on the route from London to Bury St Edmunds and Norwich.

The Crown on the west side of the A134 is a nineteenth-century building constructed around fragments of two old houses—a timbered wall and an old cellar. During the General Election of December 1885, it was the scene of a riot. This was the first poll in which all men who were householders were able to vote, irrespective of financial status. There was a single polling booth for a large area and the men of Glemsford, Lavenham and other villages were angry at having to lose a day's work in order to travel to the polling booth in Melford. Four hundred men from Glemsford arrived, headed by a band. The Tories made an attempt to intimidate the workers to vote Conservative. Soon after midday rioting began. Men, inflamed by drink, drove the owner of the Crown, a widow, to the upper rooms from which she escaped with the help of neighbours. The inn was then ransacked, window frames and furniture smashed and the few police were powerless. In the early evening the Riot Act was read by Captain Bence of Kentwell Hall and soon afterwards fifty soldiers arrived from Bury St Edmunds. The streets were cleared and order restored but only just in time, for the Crown Inn had been set on fire by the mob. The fire, however, was put out and much of the building was saved.

LOWER PEOVER, Cheshire

The Bells of Peover is approached from the B5081 which branches off the main Knutsford to Holmes Chapel road (A50). A cobbled lane leads from the village street to the Church of St Oswald which faces the inn which was founded in 1369 as a house for the priests. Since then there has been much rebuilding and until the end of the nineteenth century the inn was known as the Warren de Tabley Arms: the crest of the family with the motto *Tenebo* may still be seen on the north gable. After the death of the third and last baron—John Burne Leicester Warren—in 1895, it became The Bells of Peover, not because of any association with the church but from the family name of the licensee—Bell—whose grave is in the churchyard. The next licensee was Victoria Mabel Savage who took a pride during World War II in providing hospitality for officers of the American Army stationed nearby. General Patten stayed at the inn and General Eisenhower was entertained there.

LUDLOW, Shropshire

The Feathers, north of the Bull Ring, was built c1603 and is known to have been an inn in 1656 though there may well have been an inn on the site in the sixteenth century. It has one of the finest timbered façades in England. There are three storeys with bays surmounted by triple gables. The upper storeys overhang and at first-floor level a balustered balcony abuts against the northern bay which projects further than the rest. The timbering, much of which is finely carved, encloses diamond-shaped lozenges of plasterwork on the second storey and cusped lozenges in the shape of a cross on the second. The gables have rounded arches of timberwork.

The interior has some fine early features, particularly plaster ceilings. There is a most interesting panelled room on the first floor, now used as a lounge. The ceiling carries a moulded centrepiece with the royal arms and supporters of James I surrounded by scrolls of oak, rose, vine and thistle. There is a magnificent carved mantelpiece above the stone fireplace which has an iron fireback with the arms of Queen Elizabeth. The mantel also has the royal arms and supporters of James I, with the Tudor rose. It is probable that the name The Feathers derives from the celebrations held in Ludlow in 1616 when the office of Prince of Wales was created and the people showed 'The Love of Wales to their Sovereign Prince'.

MARKET HARBOROUGH, Leicestershire

The Three Swans in this market town of the 'hunting shires' is a three-storey seventeenth-century building which appears to have started as The Swan, an inn which issued trade tokens in 1651 and 1667. Later it became a coaching inn. An obituary of William Chapman (1802-74) states that he 'was employed at the Three Swans as helper, post-boy, chaise driver and then ostler for 60 years'.

In the early days of railways the inn declined and had to

wait until 1935 to be restored by John Fothergill who continued to run the Three Swans until 1952.[28] The most notable feature is the magnificent wrought-iron sign.

MARLBOROUGH, Wiltshire

The Castle and Ball in the High Street was originally built in Tudor times and largely rebuilt after two disastrous fires in Marlborough in 1654 which burned down much of the town. The frontage was then set back from the street and a pillared colonnade was created which Pepys described as 'penthouses supported by pillars' when he visited the town in 1668. The inn has three storeys and three gables; the upper storeys are tile-hung. Until 1764 the house was called The Antelope. It then became the Castle and Ball, though this is possibly a corruption of Castle and Bull, two of the charges in the arms of Marlborough which were depicted in a seventeenth-century trade token. Lettered signs announce the name on the tile hung frontage and on the colonnade.

The inn has always been on the main London road; in the seventeenth century it no doubt enjoyed some of the trade resulting from the races which were held on Barton Down and in the eighteenth century catered for the coaching traffic on the route to fashionable Bath. The Marlborough coach did the journey from the King's Arms, Snow Hill, London, in twelve hours, a distance of 74 miles, and passengers would often break the journey and stay for several days at the Castle and Ball. It is recorded that the elder Pitt, after he had become the Earl of Chatham and was suffering from ill health, stayed at the inn and was so demanding that the life of the house revolved around this peevish old man throughout his stay. He even forced the servants to wear the Chatham livery.

The Sun, formerly the Rising Sun, lies at the western end of the High Street, at the corner of Hyde Lane. This escaped the seventeenth-century fires and is the oldest surviving inn in the town. The frontage has been ruined by a Victorian lean-to projection on the ground floor and bay window additions to the first floor, but the roof with its three dormer windows gives some indication of its age. Inside there are many pre-

Elizabethan features including old timbers, some panelling and an old doorway which leads to the cellars.

MERE, Wiltshire

The Old Ship on the A303 was built early in the seventeenth century as a private mansion for Sir John Coventry, a staunch cavalier who sat in the Long Parliament (1640). It is a two-storey stone building with mullioned cross windows in the upper storey, a fine stone archway, and a stone-slab roof with sky-lights. It became an inn early in the eighteenth century, catering for coach traffic on the London to Exeter road and for race-goers to Mere Down in the 1730s, stabling some of the race-horses. It was called 'At the sign of the Ship'. Its fine wrought-iron sign was made by Kingston Avery, a local clockmaker, some time between 1730 and 1763. From it hangs a bunch of gilded grapes (vintner's sign). Inside the inn are beamed rooms, old stone fireplaces, an elmwood staircase which leads to the upstairs dining room and some early plasterwork ceilings in the bedrooms.

The Talbot, opposite the Old Ship, was built in the seventeenth century when it was known as the George. On Sunday, 5 October 1651 Charles II dined at the inn when travelling from Trent to Heale House, some 6 miles north of Salisbury. His party consisted of Colonel Robert Phelips with his servant, Henry Peters, Miss Juliana Coningsby, and Charles himself diguised as her groom. Fortunately the landlord was known to Phelips as a loyal royalist though the identity of the groom was not revealed.

The inn carries a sign showing a black hound; most inns with the sign of the Talbot show a white hound.

MIDHURST, Sussex

The Spread Eagle consists of two buildings of different dates fused into a single unit. The older part is half-timbered and has an overhanging second storey with lattice windows, It dates from 1430. The later part was built in 1650 of stone and brick. It has three main storeys, the third with dormer windows. Slightly below street level it has a room now known as the

Coal Hole. When the second part was built in the seventeenth century the first part had been let as shops. It has been restored relatively recently and now forms part of the hotel. Inside there are public rooms with large open fireplaces and heavy oak beams.

The name 'Spread Eagle' derives from the crest of the de Bohuns, medieval Lords of Coudreye (Cowdray). In Elizabethan days the land around was forested—the name Midhurst means 'in the midst of woodlands'. Here the queen and her lords went hunting and returned after the chase to feast at the Spread Eagle.

In the eighteenth century it became a coaching inn and travellers who spent Christmas there booked a place in the inn for the following Christmas by reserving a pudding. This custom continues and in the dining room the bookings for Christmas hang from a beam above the tables.

The Spread Eagle was greatly approved by Hilaire Belloc who described it in *The Four Men* (1912) as 'that old and most revered of all the prime inns of this world'.

MINLEY, Hampshire

The Crown and Cushion in this small village south of Hartford Bridge Flats, about 3 miles west of Camberley, consists of some seventeenth-century cottages converted into an inn. It is associated with Colonel Blood, an adventurer whose home was on the edge of Yately Common. In May 1671 he entered the Tower of London with accomplices and they succeeded in stealing the crown and the orb from the Crown Jewels. However, they were pursued and Blood was arrested in the little inn not far from his home. Later, through the good offices of Buckingham he was pardoned by Charles II and his estate of £500 a year was restored. The name of the inn derives from this incident and there is a yew tree in the inn garden shaped to represent a crown on a cushion.

MINSTEAD, Hampshire

The Trusty Servant stands by the village green in this New Forest village. The sign is a copy of an oil painting in Winchester College. It shows a creature with the head of a pig, its snout closed with a padlock, stags feet, and human hands, one of which holds an implement. The sign also bears the same words as the picture:

A Trusty Servant's portrait would you see,
This emblematic figure well survey ;
The porker's snout, not nice in diet, shows
The padlock shut, no secrets he'll disclose.
Patient the ass, his master's wrath will bear,
Swiftness in errand, the stag's feet declare.
Loaded his left hand, apt to labour saith
The vest his neatness, open hand his faith,
Girt with his sword, his shield upon his arm,
Himself and master he'll protect from harm.

The original painting is said to have been done in 1579. The picture to be seen in Winchester College today was painted by W. Cave in 1809 with the Trusty Servant in Georgian costume. The version below is from an earlier drawing of about 1700.

MORETON-IN-MARSH, Gloucestershire

The White Hart Royal in the High Street is a half-timbered building which appears to have been three houses of fourteenth- or fifteenth-century date. Most of the present Cotswold-stone construction is sixteenth century (see p 89). Charles I spent a night in the north wing in July 1644 while on a journey from Oxford to Evesham. There have been several changes since then. The entrance is now within the old archway used by horses in posting days. A ballroom was added early in the nineteenth century and above the entrance is a royal arms carrying the royal coat with red and blue ensigns in the background. This was made for a Moreton tentmaker who undertook government contracts in Victorian times. When he died and the business closed the landlord of the White Hart acquired it as a curiosity.

The interior of the inn has an interesting old balustered staircase, moulded ceiling beams, and a fine open hearth. The 'Royal' suffix is relatively recent.

MOULSFORD, Berkshire

The Beetle and Wedge is close to the A329. At Moulsford there is a side road called Ferry Lane which leads down to the River Thames and is probably the point where the old Ridgway crossed the river. It is a public landing place. It is not surprising therefore, that there should be an inn here—an attractive brick building now frequented by the owners of river boats. Its main claim to fame, however, is that H. G. Wells made it his Potwell Inn of *The History of Mr Polly* (1910).

The name of the inn derives from the implements used for splitting timber. The beetle is a heavy wooden mallet which is used to drive the wedge into the wood.

NEWARK-ON-TRENT, Nottinghamshire

The Clinton Arms in the Market Square was mainly built in the eighteenth century on the site of an inn which, over the years, had many names including The Talbot, The Cardinal's Hat, The King's Arms (from the sixteenth century), and the Kingston Arms (early nineteenth century). Lord Byron, who stayed at the inn in 1806 and 1807 when volumes of his poems were being printed in Newark, wrote: 'The Kingston Arms is my inn'. Shortly afterwards it became The Clinton Arms, taken from the family name of the Dukes of Newcastle and Earls of Lincoln who owned part of the borough. In the nineteenth century it was a noted posting establishment. The Duke of Wellington stayed at the inn on his way to Doncaster races and W. E. Gladstone addressed the electors of Newark from its balcony during the election of 1832 when he was returned as Conservative member in the first parliament elected under the the Reform Bill.

The present building has a pillared colonnade and part of the old yard is now covered-in with a glass roof to form an Edwardian-style 'Palm Court'.

The colonnade continues along the side of the square where the yard entrance to the former **Saracen's Head** now forms a public right of way. This was the coaching inn in which Jeannie Dean (Scott's *Heart of Midlothian*) stayed on her way to London in 1733. Still further along the same side of the square it is possible to see the carved and painted timbers of what was once the fourteenth-century **White Hart.**

NEWBY BRIDGE, Lancashire

The Swan is close to the fine old grey stone bridge of five arches which crosses the River Leven as it leaves Lake Windermere and flows south to Morecambe Bay, a strategic position for an inn. There was certainly one on the site in the sixteenth century. The Swan today is a large old coaching house of three main storeys and a slate roof with dormer windows. It faces the bridge and there is an effigy sign of a white horse above the main entrance. In 1855 Nathaniel Hawthorne described his journey by coach from Milnthorpe Station to the Swan at Newby Bridge 'which sits low and well sheltered in the lap of the hills—an old fashioned inn where the landlord and his people have a simple and friendly way of dealing with their guests'.

The hotel has 300yd of river frontage where there is fishing for brown trout, sea trout and, after July, salmon.

NEWMARKET, Suffolk

The Rutland Arms was designed by William Kent and built on the site of the former Royal Palace of Newmarket c1740. It is a large two-storey building of brick with a decorative cornice and pediments on two sides. The longer frontage faces the main street and has a pillared portico; the shorter side faces east and has a large coaching archway leading to the central yard. For many years the inn was owned by the Duke of Rutland, hence its name.

The Rutland Arms has a sporting tradition. R. S. Surtees describes how Mr Jorrocks and the Yorkshireman when staying in the inn noticed that 'most of the inmates of the house were up with the lark to early exercise'. In 1831 Squire George Osbaldstone, a small man only 5ft tall and probably the greatest sportsman of all time, already forty-five years of age, announced his intention to beat the record of Dick Turpin's ten-hour ride from London to York. Colonel Charritie bet him one thousand guineas that he would not succeed and a 200-mile round course was pegged out on Newmarket Heath. Despite a fall, Osbaldstone succeeded in covering the course in nine hours. He then went straight to the Rutland Arms, took a hot bath, and began to celebrate his achievement. 'I'm so hungry I could eat an old woman' he said as he started an eating and drinking session which lasted nearly to dawn.

There are dozens of stories associated with the inn. One of the most remarkable concerns the Earl of Oxford who drove a chariot drawn by a team of tame stags from Houghton Hall in Norfolk. Suddenly the stags were pursued by a pack of hounds into Newmarket where they were guided into the courtyard of the Rutland Arms and the gates were closed just in time to avoid disaster.

The list of sportsmen who have used the inn is unending and includes Admiral Henry Rous, Fred Archer, Sir Gordon Richards and Steve Donoghue.

NORTON ST PHILIP, Somerset

The George was built as a hospice by the Carthusian Priory of Hinton. It served also as a storehouse for the local wool trade; the Carthusian monks were themselves sheep farmers. An account of the foundation at Hinton is given in E. M. Thompson's book on *The Carthusian Order in England* (1930).

The original stone building dates from 1397 but a fire destroyed the upper part and only the ground floor remains. The upper storeys were rebuilt, probably about 1500 or a little earlier. These are half-timbered and overhang, and there are three oriel windows on the first floor. The ground floor has two canted stone bays to the left of the arched entrance. To the right a flight of stone steps leads to a platform and a doorway well above street level (see p 89). Pevsner refers to this as 'later' than the rest of the ground floor but does not ascribe a date.[29] It would seem that this might have been a loading platform for waggons carrying cloth or wool. Wool was certainly stored in the building ready for the annual fair on the feast of St Philip and St James.

The George was used by Cromwell and his men during the Civil War. During the Rebellion after the Battle of Norton Philip and before Sedgemoor, an attempt was made to kill the Duke of Monmouth when he was staying in the inn on 26 June 1685. A shot was fired from the street when he was at an upper window but failed to find its mark. No doubt the attacker was trying to win the £1,000 that had been offered by King James to anyone who succeeded in killing Monmouth. Later in that year Judge Jeffreys stayed at the George during his Bloody Assize.

NORWICH, Norfolk

The Bell in Orford Hill near the Market Place was an inn at the end of the sixteenth century when it was known as the Blue Bell. Some carved oak beams are all that remain of this period. There is, however, a good Georgian staircase and the entrance in the relatively modern three-storey castellated frontage once led to a courtyard which has been roofed over and incorporated in the building.

The Bell has always been a local inn. Until well into the 1700s it was noted for cockfighting. In the 1750s the landlord was a bit of a rebel, a lively character who could not abide puritanism or authority. During his tenure a 'Hell Fire Club' met at the inn which consisted of local 'toughs' who tried to break up the meetings held by the Wesleys and tormented their followers.

In the nineteenth century the house was more law-abiding. It was here that 'the Loyal and Constitutional Club' was founded in 1831. The old minute books reveal that the Duke of Wellington was one of the original members.

The Maid's Head at the corner of Magdalen Street dates from the late thirteenth century when it was called Molde Fish Tavern or Murtel Fish Tavern.[30] The name was changed before 1472 to the Mayd's Hedde so it has no connection with Queen Elizabeth's visit to the city. The present building has 'mock Tudor' gables and timbering but inside there is a genuine early fireplace with stone ingle seats and some excellent Jacobean woodwork.

In the seventeenth century the inn became a coaching terminus and as traffic increased in the eighteenth century it virtually became the civic centre. Every possible type of local activity took place within the inn—banquets, venison feasts, concerts, lectures and even exhibitions of flowers. In 1724 the first Freemason Lodge in Norwich was formed at the Maid's Head and met in the inn for many years.

In 1762 the 'Norwich Machine' left the Maid's Head Inn for the Green Dragon in Bishopsgate, London, three times a week, at half past eleven in the forenoon, arriving in London on the evening of the following day.

NOTTINGHAM

The Flying Horse in Poultry, close to the Market Place, carries the date 1483. Perhaps this was the date when the building became an inn for the original building was a private house rebuilt in 1392, belonging to the Plumptre family. It was certainly an inn in Tudor times though little of the earlier building remains. A reconstruction in the 1930s produced an impressive gabled façade said to be a faithful reproduction of the Tudor frontage.

The inn has always been a meeting place. In the eighteenth

Page 125: *(above)* Adam-style assembly room, The Lion, Shrewsbury; *(below)* The Dolphin, Southampton

Page 126: King Henry V Court Room, The Red Lion, Southampton

century it was the headquarters of the Tory party. In 1818 Thomas Assheton Smith (who was Master of the Quorn Hunt in 1805) used it as his committee room in an unsuccessful campaign in a parliamentary election.

Stage people have often used the Flying Horse. Paul Bedford, the famous vocalist and comedian, stayed there in 1849 when it was kept by William Malpas, a local iron and steel merchant.

The name of the inn is almost certainly derived from an ancient swinging horse which entertained the crowds at medieval fairs. A rider mounted on the horse swung to and fro trying to take a ring from a quintain with a sword. The illustration is from a drawing made c1720.

Ye Olde Trip to Jerusalem in Castle Road, at the foot of the cliff which rises to Nottingham Castle, boldly claims to be the oldest inn in England. It carries the date AD 1189, the year of the Crusades and it is said that a group of crusaders encamped outside the castle to refresh themselves at this tavern. Most of the present brick and timber building is no more than 250 years old though part of the inn has always been a cavern cut from the soft brown sandstone of the cliff.

ODIHAM, Hampshire

The George in the High Street is in part a Tudor building; the date of the first licence is often given as 1547. Much of the original timbered structure remains and may be seen from the back and inside the inn. The frontage, however, dates from Georgian times when it was an important coaching inn. The dining room has Tudor panelling and a carved Elizabethan chimneypiece which was rescued from Basing House after its siege and destruction by Cromwell's forces during the Civil War. This room was once used as a manorial court and sentenced prisoners could be dealt with on the spot—whipped or taken to the cells below. The whipping post which was used for debtors and nagging wives is still in place in No 5 bedroom. The cells were used for French prisoners during the Napoleonic Wars. Later the magistrates' court used the inn which has been a meeting place in the town for many years.

In the eighteenth century the Odiham Agricultural Society met at the George. In 1782, after the Hambledon Cricket Club had played a match at Odiham, the landlord of the George gave a silver punch ladle to the cricket club which sang the best three songs, and a spoon to the best solo singer.

Early in the nineteenth century a field at the back of the inn was the scene of many prize fights. Tom Sayers was particularly noted for his prowess. A framed 'Programme of Entertainment' hangs in the bar, marking his 'Farewell to the Ring' when he was introduced to the audience 'in private costume with medals'. In the programme is printed a poem which it is supposed he wrote himself. It starts:

The first I beat was Aby Crouch, 'twas only for £10:
The next I beat Dan Collins in four and twenty rounds.
For £100 I beat Jack Grant in eighteen hundred and fifty two
And in eighteen hundred and fifty three I beat Jack Martin too.

Thus his whole career is covered in many verses until the last event before retirement in 1860:

My last fight was with Heenan who from America came;
I never fought a better man nor one who showed more game.
For two long hours and better each tried his best to win
And none could tell which man was beat when the ring was broken in.

This last fight with John Camel Heenan, the Benicia Boy, took place on 17 April 1860, in a Hampshire meadow only a few miles from the George, both fighters having journeyed to Farnborough from London to escape from the police.

OSWESTRY, Shropshire

The Wynnstay in Church Street, opposite the Parish Church, was originally the Cross Foxes and in 1825 became the Wynnstay Arms. It was built in the eighteenth century to cater for the coaching and posting traffic of the Holyhead Road. The three-storey brick building with a fine four-pillar portico has always been closely associated with the Welsh family of Williams Wynn of Wynnstay. The original Cross Foxes referred to the two red foxes in their coat-of-arms. These can still be seen in a glass lantern light above the portico and also, together with eagles which also appear in the Wynnstay coat-of-arms, in the moulded plasterwork of a first floor lounge which once formed part of a larger assembly hall. In 1769 an ox was roasted in front of the inn to celebrate the wedding of a member of the Wynn family.

The inn was a stopping place for the Holyhead mail coaches and a post office was established there in 1809. In 1832 the Duchess of Kent and her daughter, Victoria, stayed at the Wynnstay Arms. James Knight, the landlord, must have had an anxious time for such large crowds flocked to the decorated town to celebrate the occasion that a woman was killed in the crush.

The Wynnstay has always been noted for its bowling green, now well over 200 years old, and still in use.

OUNDLE, Northamptonshire

The Talbot in this small town on the River Nene, carries the date 1626 on its gold and black metal sign but it occupies a site where there has been a hostelry since 638. The original, known as the Tabret, was attached to a monastery built by Bishop Wilfred. The seventeenth-century date marks the complete restoration and rebuilding of an older house. Some of the repairs were done with stone from Fotheringhay Castle, and the panelling in the lounge and the main staircase was from the same source.

The hotel is of three storeys and has bays with mullioned windows reaching from ground level to gables on either side of the central archway which leads to the yard and the entrance. The gables are decorated with stone ball finials at both base and apex.

The Talbot is much used by parents of boys in residence at Oundle Public School which was founded in 1556.

OXFORD

The Golden Cross in Cornmarket Street is on the site of a building erected by the canons of Osney Abbey and sold in the reign of Richard I to a wine merchant. It was then made into an inn though it appears to have retained some ecclesiastical significance. Manger, Bishop of Worcester in the twelfth century, was born in the building. The inn was later (c1390) bought by William of Wykeham for New College. Parts of the present building date from the fifteenth century. Latimer and Ridley slept at the inn in 1555 and Cranmer in 1556. The Lord Lieutenant of Oxford stayed here when he proclaimed James II king. When William III was made king, William Lovelace with 400 troopers visited Oxford to proclaim the succession and he also stayed at the Golden Cross.

The inn is approached through an old coaching entrance which leads to a cobbled courtyard. Six original oriel windows can be seen on the right as one looks outward towards the street. The bay windows on the ground floor are probably eighteenth century. Now, full of grillrooms and bars, the building no longer retains the true character of an old inn.

The Mitre in the High Street has vaulted stone cellars now used as wine vaults which suggest an early date for the original building, probably c1230. The main building today, with three gables, each with an oriel window dates from the seventeenth century. (One gable bears the date 1631.) The frontage is mainly eighteenth century.

For over 200 years the Mitre was a coaching inn. In 1671 a

'good coach and able horses' set forth for London 'every Tuesday, Thursday and Saturday. Performed if God permit'.

The inn was for a long period a favourite for staff and for students of the university. In the days when 'Town and Gown' were at loggerheads it appears to have been the favoured base of the academics. Today, like the Golden Cross, the Mitre no longer has the atmosphere of an old coaching inn.

PENRITH, Cumberland

The Gloucester Arms in Great Dockray is the oldest inn building in Penrith. According to tradition this was originally Dockray Hall, the residence (c1471) of Richard, Duke of Gloucester who became King Richard III. Over the entrance is a carved and emblazoned shield bearing his coat of arms with white boars as supporters. Richard used the boar as a badge before he came to the throne. In 1580 extensive alterations were made by John Whelpdale. The inn is built of stone, now faced with painted stucco. Inside there are original plaster ceilings with the ducal arms and some fifteenth-century panelling.

The Hussar in King Street is an old posting house where the stage coaches from London changed horses for their journey over the border. In those days it was known as The Crown and later as Siddle's Crown Hotel. The Georgian façade of three storeys has a central pillared entrance and on either side there are Victorian bay windows. It is said that one of the first presentations of the Lonsdale Belt was made in the ballroom of the Crown.

The Robin Hood carries a plaque erected by the Penrith Urban District Council, bearing the words: 'William Wordsworth stayed here with Raisley Calvert 1794-5'. Raisley Calvert was the brother of William Calvert, an old school-fellow of Wordsworth at Hawkshead School. They were the sons of the steward of the Duke of Norfolk who owned a large estate at Greystone, 4 miles from Penrith. When Wordsworth stayed with Raisley Calvert at the Robin Hood Inn he was no doubt concerned for his sick friend who was consumptive. In fact Wordsworth nursed Raisley for a time in William Calvert's farmhouse, Windy Brow, which stood on the south slope of Latrigg, near

Keswick. Raisley died in January 1795 and left Wordsworth a legacy of £900.

RAMPSIDE, Lancashire

The Concle Inn in this little village close to the shore of Morecambe Bay, at the southern extremity of Furness, is an undistinguished public house with a curious name. It was once known as the Bay Horse and in the seventeenth century, schooners used to tie up at the nearby wharf. The inn changed its name in the middle of the nineteenth century when this strip of coast became a minor resort. A contemporary account describes Rampside as 'frequently visited in the summer season by genteel company for the purpose of bathing in the Conckhole which, in the absence of the tide, is always filled with a dense saline fluid, and is much extolled for its peculiar advantages.'

RIPLEY, Surrey

The Anchor, at one time The Old George, is on the east side of the High Street. It is a small, many gabled brick and timber building which dates, in part, from 1256. It gained a reputation in the 1890s as a port of call when the road between Kingston and Guildford became a popular stretch for cyclists in the days of the 'penny-farthing'. It continued as a haven for cyclists until World War I, for they were not always welcomed at wayside inns. The hosts at this time were Annie and Harriet Dibble, and the vicar of the church which lies behind the inn allowed the cyclists to park their machines on church land. Roughly 24 miles from Hyde Park Corner, the Anchor made a reasonable afternoon's run for Londoners. The tradition continued into the motor cycle age.

The Talbot, on the same side of the High Street, is an ivy-covered brick building with a high central archway leading to the old yard. The inn was established in 1453 and parts of the structure date back to this period. Until 1636, and probably even later, it was known as The Dog. Claud Duval, the highwayman, is said to have used a bedroom at the Talbot from which he could escape by way of a chimney and rear door if pursued.

In the eighteenth century the inn became an important port of call on the coaching road to Portsmouth. It was used, though involuntarily, by Admiral Byng when he was taken to be court-martialled at Portsmouth before he was shot on the quarter deck of the *Monarque* on 14 March 1757.

Lord Nelson and Lady Hamilton used the Talbot when travelling to Portsmouth many years later.

ROCHESTER, Kent

The Crown, near the bridge across the Medway, is the oldest inn in Rochester and was built in 1316 as the Hospital of St Catherine to care for the poor. In 1390 it became a manorial inn owned by Simon Potyn who was several times member of parliament for the city. It was in the Crown Inn that Henry VIII first set eyes on Anne of Cleves. On 18 September 1573, Queen Elizabeth arrived at the inn and stayed four days. Shakespeare may well have known it for it is said that the inn yard was the one where the flea-bitten carriers tried to borrow a lantern (*King Henry V*, Part II). In May 1732 William Hogarth went to the Crown with his 'four merry companions' (Scott Tothall, Thornhill and Forrest) where they dined

> . . . on a dish of soles and flounders with crab sauce, a calf's head stuffed and roasted, the liver fried and other appurtenances minced, all very good and well drest with good small beer and excellent port.

As a result of the visit Forrest wrote a description of Rochester which was illustrated by Hogarth and Scott.

In 1836 the Crown changed hands and, taking the name of its new owner, became **Wright's**, the inn referred to by Jingle in *Pickwick Papers* (1836-7) as

> . . . dear-very-dear, half a crown on the bill if you look at the waiter—charge you more if you dine at a friend's than they would if you dined in the coffee-room—rum fellows—very.

Until 1863 the High Street frontage carried the original fourteenth-century gables and bargeboards but these disappeared during the rebuilding in that year. For some time after this it was known as the Royal Crown Hotel. Apart from the crypt, there is little today to remind one of its romantic past. The two-storey building of blackened yellow brick should be viewed from the relative quiet of Gundulph Square; at this end of the High Street traffic thunders across the Medway Bridge in an incessant stream and anyone trying to view the Crown from the road is taking his life in his hands.

The King's Head in the High Street dates from the seventeenth century though it may well have been a hospice on the London to Canterbury road as early as 1490. It is recorded that Charles II stayed at the inn.

In the eighteenth century the King's Head was partly rebuilt. The main changes were made in 1790 when it had become an important coaching centre on the Dover road. Still further rebuilding in the nineteenth century resulted in the present rather unattractive frontage with the upper storeys covered in stucco and the ground floor walls with dark brown tiles. However, some earlier features can still be seen including a fine Georgian staircase.

Some authorities consider the King's Head to be the original of The Winglebury Arms in 'the Great Winglebury Duel' in Charles Dickens' collected papers—*Sketches by Boz* (1836).

The Royal Victoria and Bull, formerly The Bull, is in the High Street, opposite the Guildhall erected by John Bryan in 1687. It was an important eighteenth-century coaching house on the Dover road (the old Roman Watling Street), built of brick and with a large yard which provided stabling for many horses. Evidence of the old gallery can be traced in the corridors to the bedrooms.

The inn was often visited by Charles Dickens who is known to have used Room 17. This is The Bull of *Pickwick Papers* (1836-7) and the Blue Boar of *Great Expectations* (1860-1). Mr Jingle referred to it in *Pickwick Papers* as 'a good house, nice beds'. The ball attended by Tracy Tupman was held in the assembly room. It has a minstrel's gallery which carries the royal arms of Queen Victoria who stayed in the Bull as Princess Victoria with her mother, the Duchess of Kent, on 29 November 1836, when a storm had damaged the bridge across the Medway.

ROMSEY, Hampshire

The White Horse in the Cornmarket has a Georgian brick frontage which hides a much earlier building. In the twelfth century it was the guest house for Romsey Abbey. The stone cellars reveal early work which was clearly renovated in Tudor times—a Gothic window and part of the entrance to an underground passage leading to the abbey.

After the dissolution of the monasteries in the reign of Henry VIII, the earlier building was pulled down and a new one was built as an inn. Its Tudor origins have revealed themselves over the years. Some years ago a large wall painting was uncovered. It is in the form of black Tudor roses linked by a curved geometric design. This was carefully restored and is safely preserved. The most recent discoveries were in 1961 when Tudor strap-work design paintings were found on the wattle and daub of the timbered walls in the lounge. These old grisaille panels must at one time have formed a dado round the room. They were carefully restored by the artist and medieval expert Miss Elsie Matley Moore (see p 90).

In 1776 the White Horse was a galleried inn providing thirty-five beds for guests and stabling for fifty horses. In 1793 the London coach set out from the inn every day, and the Southampton—Bristol coach called daily except Sundays. In 1800, Joseph Phillips, the landlord, enclosed the galleries by windows to keep out the weather and they now form a corridor to the bedrooms. The fine eighteenth-century staircase leading to these rooms has a lower banister carved from a single piece of timber.

ROSS-ON-WYE, Herefordshire

The Royal Hotel in Palace Pound is on the site of a former palace of the Bishops of Hereford overlooking a horseshoe bend of the River Wye. The hotel was built in 1837 and it was provided with a large stable yard to cater for the coaching traffic. In the cellars there is a foundation stone laid by a local Freemason's lodge. It was opened by James Barrett who had previously been the landlord of an inn called the Swan.

Charles Dickens met his friend, John Forster, in the Royal in 1867 when they discussed the possibility that Dickens might undertake a lecture tour in America. Forster was against it but in the end Dickens went and the tour proved to be a great success.

Queen Victoria stayed in the hotel before her accession to the throne as did Queen Mary when she was Princess Victoria Mary of Teck.

RYE, Sussex

The Bell in the Mint at the western end of the High Street was built in the fifteenth century and still has some original timbering. It was used by smugglers, particularly by the Hawkhurst Gang in the middle of the eighteenth century. At one time a tunnel connected it with the cellars of the Mermaid Inn. There was also a door on the first floor which led to the house next door and a revolving cupboard on the ground floor designed so that a smuggler could step into it and then use it like a revolving door to gain access to the street.

The George in the High Street began in the Butchery opposite the Town Hall; a document of 1575 states that it was kept by Edward Bryan, a glover. It moved to a Tudor building on the present site c1739 and became the Head Inn. Some of the original beams and stone fireplaces can still be seen inside the building. A new frontage was built c1760 when the inn was enlarged, with three storeys, a tiled roof and dormer windows.

The barons of the Cinque Ports were once entertained in the Long Room on the first floor. When a new mayor is elected it has always been customary for him to throw hot pennies from the Long Room balcony to the crowd below. It was a Whig house and when the election results produced a Whig victory it would be celebrated in the George.

In 1850 a prodigious banquet of fifty-seven courses was held when Thomas Farncomb, the Lord Mayor of London, visited Rye for the opening of the railway. The menu can still be seen in the hotel. The George is mentioned in Sheila Kaye-Smith's novel *Sussex Gorse* (1916).

The Mermaid is one of the oldest and finest inns in England. It owes a great deal to the fact that it was built in a medieval walled town set on a hill. It has escaped modern 'development' and still stands in a cobbled street much as it was 500 years ago (see p 107).

The original tavern of 1300 was of wattle and daub. This was destroyed in 1377 when the French raided Rye, except for the cellars which have a barrel-vaulted ceiling hewn from the rock. In 1420 the inn was rebuilt on the main route leading to the sea through Strand Gate and has been very little changed. It is a half-timbered building with close-set uprights beneath a tiled roof with dormer windows. The upper storey overhangs.

In Elizabethan times it was a centre for feasting and celebration in the town and it is thought that the queen herself visited the Mermaid when she came to Rye in 1573. In the years that followed business flourished. In the seventeenth century Michael Cadman issued a 'Mearmeade' trade token.

The year 1614, when the export of wool was forbidden by law, marked the beginning of 'owling'—the illegal export of wool in exchange for the import of wine, brandy and tobacco. In time this smuggling became highly organised. In the eighteenth century the Hawkhurst Gang which operated in this part of Sussex became so powerful that local people were forced to co-operate and the magistrates feared to condemn them. The gang was founded by George Gray and at a later date three ruthless characters—Fairall, Kingsmill and Perrin—operated with it and openly used the Mermaid as a base for their armed forays. In 1735, Thomas Moore, a smuggler who had been released on bail, went to the inn and dragged the bailiff down the street to the harbour. Fortunately for the bailiff he was rescued by the captain of a revenue sloop which was there at anchor. Smuggling traffic continued well into the nineteenth century and inevitably the trade of the Mermaid suffered to some extent. In 1913 it was run as a club by Mrs May Aldington, mother of the novelist, Richard Aldington.

The revival of the Mermaid came with the increase in motor traffic and the publicity brought by the fact that Russell Thorndike used the inn as a setting for his *Dr Syn* novels. Notable visitors have included Ford Madox Ford, Hilaire Belloc, Henry James, Ellen Terry and Rupert Brooke.

The rooms of the Mermaid are worth careful study. The reception hall has a fine timbered ceiling supported by a king-post and there is good oak panelling on the walls. To the left is 'Dr Syn's Lounge', a room with linenfold panelling and interesting carving which includes the letters J.H.S.—*Jesus Homnium Salvator*. This dates from the Reformation when priests took refuge here on their way to the coast to cross the Channel.

The lounge bar has an enormous fireplace, and behind the beam which spans it is a priest's hole. A solid central king-post supports the ceiling beams and in one corner is a 'secret' stairway leading to a bedroom—a relic of smuggling days.

Notable features in the restaurant are two kingposts, good linenfold panelling and two Caen stone fireplaces. The bedrooms have interesting timbering and in 'Dr Syn's Bedchamber' there is a bookcase which hides the old staircase to the lounge below.

SAFFRON WALDEN, Essex

The Sunn Inn at the junction of Church Street and Market Hall is no longer an inn but is of such interest that no visitor to Saffron Walden should fail to see it. The earliest part is a hall house of the fifteenth century. There are two storeys; the upper, beneath a steep gabled roof, overhangs the lower. The frontage has extremely fine seventeenth-century parge work or pargetting. This consists of a tough plaster mixed from lime and ox-hair, moulded in this case to depict scenes from history. The plaster-work sign depicts the Sun supported by two giants.

The Sunn Inn was the headquarters of Cromwell and Fairfax in 1647. It was acquired by the National Trust in 1933 through the Ancient Buildings Trust and is now used for an office, shop and flats.

ST ALBANS, Hertfordshire

The Fighting Cocks is in Abbey Mill Lane close to the cathedral and near the little River Ver. It is a small octagonal timber-framed inn on a brick base and was probably first built early in the fourteenth century as an elaborate pigeon-house or dove-cote. Although it is often described as one of the oldest inns in

England it did not become a licensed house until it was rebuilt on its present site in 1599. The following statement appears on the inn wall:

The Old Round House
Rebuilt after the Flood
(of 1599)

The site was formerly occupied by St Germain's Gate, part of the monastery founded by King Offa of Mercia in 793. In the seventeenth and eighteenth centuries the inn became a centre for the sport of cockfighting which gave it its name. It was renamed The Fisherman when the sport was made illegal in 1849 but has since reverted to the earlier description.

The Fighting Cocks was restored in 1971.

The White Hart, formerly the Hartshorn, in Holywell Hill, was built in the fifteenth or the early sixteenth century. It is a half-timbered inn with close-set uprights and a tiled roof with dormer windows. Inside there are fine old beams and one room has a minstrel gallery. When the inn was restored in 1928 some medieval wall paintings were revealed and these are now preserved.

In 1746 Lord Lovat stayed at the White Hart with his captors after the Battle of Culloden when he was being taken to the Tower of London. He was later executed for his part in the Jacobite Rising. It was here that Hogarth painted the portrait of Lovat which is now in the National Portrait Gallery.

Lady Grosvenor stayed at the White Hart when travelling to London from the north and met the Duke of Cumberland, a meeting which gave rise to a lawsuit. In 1770 Richard, Lord Grosvenor brought an action against the duke when the landlady and chambermaid were called as witnesses.

SALISBURY, Wiltshire

The Chough in Blue Boar Row is a seventeenth-century inn (c1635) on the northern side of the Market Place. It was formerly called the Cornishe Choffe Inne. The Chough is a seabird now restricted to parts of Cornwall and Wales though until the nineteenth century it was also found on the cliffs of Kent. It has a prominent beak and red legs. The inn is not far distant from the church of St Thomas of Canterbury and there is little doubt that the name 'Chough' has affiliations with Canterbury. The arms of Archbishop Thomas Becket were:

Argent	Three Choughs Sable	Beckit and Leggit	Gules
(Silver)	(Black)	(Beak and Legs)	(Red)

Inside the inn there is a fine staircase with turned balusters. At one time there were extensive stables which were used for horses until 1920. They have since been converted to form a bar and skittle alley.

The George in the High Street is no longer a licensed house. The ground floor of the old building was removed in 1967 and a steel frame was inserted to support the upper floors. It now serves as the entrance to a shopping precinct known as the Old George Mall, There is, however, still much to be seen of this very fine old inn. It was built in 1314 as a hospice for pilgrims and was owned by the Teynterer family from c1320 until 1378 when William Teynterer left it to his wife Alesia. In 1410 her second husband, George Meriot, died and orders were given that it should be sold. In 1414 it was bought by the city corporation under a licence from Henry IV and the city owned it until 1863 when the license lapsed. Part of the old fifteen-century frontage is still intact with the bays installed in 1453. Fortunately the great hall can still be seen as it forms part of the adjoining restaurant which has an upper floor called The Old George Room. There are massive constructional timbers including scissor braces, tie beams and kingposts with a fifteenth-century hammerbeam roof. There are fine fireplaces and some early plasterwork. Carved heads in the beams are of Edward II and his Queen Isabella.

The courtyard of the old inn, now absorbed in the shopping centre, was used for theatrical performances and it is said that Shakespeare came here with his players. In 1624 it was the only inn in Salisbury where itinerant players were allowed.

Cromwell slept in the George Inn on 17 October 1645 when

on the way to join his army, and Samuel Pepys on 10 June 1668. His diary records:

> Come to the George Inne, where lay in a silk bed ; and a very good diet but next day on paying the reckoning, it was to exhorbitant. I was mad and resolved to trouble the mistress about it and got something for the poor and came away in that humour.

Dickens mentions the George in *Martin Chuzzlewit* (1843).

The Haunch of Venison in Minster Street near the Poultry Cross is an old three-storey building which dates from about 1320 and became a chophouse in the eighteenth century. The bar has black oak timbers and there are pewter taps which yield the port and sherry. It is said that during alterations in the eighteenth century a marked playing card and a man's hand were found in a baking oven, a sharp reminder of the penalty a man could pay for attempting to cheat at cards. The inn was used by Augustus John when he came to Salisbury.

The King's Arms in St John Street is timber-framed with four storeys of which the upper two overhang. The spaces between the timbers are filled with wattle and daub and one section of the plasterwork has been removed on the frontage to show the use of this material; it is now protected from the weather by a glass panel.

In the mid-seventeenth century the inn was kept by a landlord called Hewitt who allowed the Royalists to use it as a secret rendezvous during the summer of 1651 when Charles II lay concealed at Heale House, some 3 miles away.

Lord Wilmot and Henry Peters, a faithful servant of Colonel Francis Wyndham of Trent, found secure asylum at the King's Arms on 24 September 1651 and with the help of Dr Humphrey Henchman who lived in the Cathedral Close, laid plans for the king's escape to France.[31]

The inn later became a coaching centre and there is still a fine timbered yard entrance. Above one of the doors of the High Street frontage is an angel carved in wood.

The Red Lion in Milford Street was established in the fifteenth century and later became a coaching inn on the route from

London to the Westcountry. The three-storey stucco frontage is Georgian. The unusually high coaching entrance leads through a double set of gates (wood and iron) to a fine old yard hung with Virginia creeper. Here stands an effigy sign of a red lion and in the entrance hall there is a remarkable organ and skeleton clock.

The White Hart which dominates St John Street was built on the site of an earlier inn which is thought to have existed in the reign of Henry VII. In 1618 when King James I came to Sarum to meet Sir Walter Raleigh after the failure of his expedition to Guiana, Sir Walter was already in a lodging in the city. He arrived there on 27 July with his wife, Sir Lewis Studeley and Manourie, a Frenchman who pretended to be knowledgeable about medicine. Fearing the king's early arrival Raleigh realised that he must gain time to prepare a defence, so he feigned sickness and later insanity. By using unguents prepared by Manourie he induced the symptoms of leprosy. Three local physicians were called in and pronounced his condition incurable. At all events, he gained his respite. Each night he worked hard on his *Apology for the Voyage to Guiana* but his exertions after publicly refusing food produced an acute hunger and, according to the chronicler, 'Manourie accordingly procured from The White Hart Inn a leg of mutton and some loaves which Raleigh devoured in secret and thus led his attendants to suppose that he took no kind of sustenance'. Although the court arrived before he left Salisbury, he did not see the king.

On 9 October 1780 Henry Laurens, sometime President of the American Congress, was brought to the White Hart on his way to London having been captured at sea on 5 September in the *Mercury Packet* bound from Philadelphia to Holland. She was intercepted by the *Vestal* and *Fury* ships of war on the Banks of Newfoundland. Subsequently Laurens spent fourteen months in the Tower of London.

The present White Hart brick building of three storeys was erected c1800. The frontage is most impressive (see p 108). A portecochère, added in 1820, projects across the pavement. Above this is a balcony with four massive Ionic pillars supporting

Page 143: *(above)* Elizabethan wall paintings in The White Swan, Stratford-upon-Avon; *(below)* The Bell, Thetford

Page 144: *(above)* The Rose and Crown, Tonbridge; *(below)* The White Hart, Whitchurch

a pediment at roof level. A large white hart in effigy was placed on this pediment in 1827 to rival the sign of the Antelope, another Salisbury inn.

The White Hart is referred to in *Martin Chuzzlewit*. It was here that Martin and Tom Pinch were entertained to dinner by John Westlock.

SANDWICH, Kent

The King's Arms is a two-storey stucco building with a tiled roof. The upper storey overhangs and reveals the fact that the inn is of timber construction. There is a finely carved gargoyle on a corner corbel dated 1592 but it must be assumed that the building is earlier, otherwise it would surely have been the Queen's Arms. It was undoubtedly built when Sandwich was the centre of a flourishing woollen industry run mainly by Huguenot weavers who settled in the town towards the end of the sixteenth century. There is a fine plaster coat of arms over the doorway painted in black, red, blue and gold.

On the north side of the town in the High Street, close to the Toll Bridge and the Barbican, two early inns face one another across a side street—**The Admiral Owen** and **The Crispin.** They are both timbered with overhanging upper storeys, though most of the timbers are hidden behind plaster. Admiral Owen was the leading figure in countering the attempted French invasion in 1804; he destroyed the enemy gunboats off Boulogne.

St Crispin and his brother Crispianus were Romans who fled from persecution in the reign of Emperor Diocletian and settled in France, working as shoemakers. Here they were again forced to affirm their Christian faith and were martyred for it.

SARRE, Kent

The Crown is a whitewashed brick-built inn dating from the seventeenth century though there was an inn on the site in 1500. In 1696 it was known as The Plough and thereafter The Hare and Hounds, The Turkey and, finally The Crown. It has always been noted for its cherry brandy. The secret recipe for this is said to have been handed down from the days when it was brought to the inn by a Huguenot refugee at the end of the seventeenth century. Charles Dickens wrote part of *Bleak House* (1852-3) at the Crown which is clearly proud of its many well known patrons. On the front wall are three boards listing in all forty-five well known personalities who have visited the inn, among them Charles Dickens, George Cruikshank, Rudyard Kipling, Lord Carson, Viscount Rothermere, Lady Wyndham and some thirty people associated with the stage, including Ellen Terry, Bransby Williams and Sir Seymour Hicks.

SELBORNE, Hampshire

The Queen's was built on the site of an earlier inn called The Compasses soon after Queen Victoria came to the throne. The Compasses was a low cottage-like building which was certainly known to the famous clergyman-naturalist Gilbert White who lived close by in The Wakes where he wrote *The Natural History and Antiquities of Selborne* (1789).

In 1830 stormy meetings were held in the Compasses where the small farmers of Selborne met to discuss their grievances with the vicar's warden. There was a serious riot in the village at about this time and the Compasses was burnt down. The leader, of the riot, John Neland, who was known as The Trumpeter, is buried beneath an enormous yew tree in Selborne churchyard.

The new inn built to replace the Compasses was known for many years as the Queen's Arms. The editor of the 1853 edition of *The Natural History and Antiquities of Selborne* describes it as 'the chief inn of the place, where the visitor will be hospitably entertained'. At this time the village was already attracting many naturalists and carriages were sent from the Queen's Arms to Alton to bring visitors on the last stage of their journey.

W. H. Hudson stayed at the inn and in *Hampshire Days* (1903) describes how he watched the house martins building their nests under the eaves.

SHAFTESBURY, Dorset

The Grosvenor in the Commons has a longer history than its late Georgian frontage would suggest. It is on the site of the New Inn which belonged to Shaftesbury Abbey and certainly existed in 1533. By 1626 it had changed its name to the Red Lion and by the eighteenth century it had become the chief inn of the town. There were several other inns nearby—the Star Inn which belonged to Eton College from c1550 and the Cock Inn on the north side. The coaching trade was extensive and the Red Lion took a major share. In 1785 a hall for Dorset Quarter Sessions was built at the back though after 1822 these were held at Dorchester.

The inn was largely rebuilt in 1826 and this is possibly the date for the change of name. It is an impressive three-storey building which amalgamated with the Cock on the north side. The upper storeys overhang and are supported by six massive pillars. There is a central entrance to the old yard and above this, at roof level, is a pediment. The large windows on the first floor light the assembly room. In 1890 the Star Inn was also united with the Grosvenor.

The hotel houses the famous Chevy Chase sideboard, 12ft long and carved in solid oak. It tells the story of the Border battle of Chevy Chase at Otterburn between the Percy ancestor of the Duke of Northumberland and the Scottish Douglas family. The sideboard was carved by Gerrard Robinson of Newcastle between 1857 and 1863, a commission from the Duke of Northumberland (see p 108).

SHREWSBURY, Shropshire

The Lion in Wyle Cop stands next door to the old house in which King Henry VII lodged when he went to Bosworth field in August 1485. The inn has a frontage in three parts. In the centre is a small fifteenth-century timber-framed building which was rebuilt in eighteenth-century gothic with a 'little open gallery', as Dickens called it between the first floor windows. On either side are brick-built blocks which were added in the eigtheenth century. The left-hand block has three storeys; the right-hand block four. Here the main entrance has a Tuscan porch which carries an effigy sign of a lion rampant, paw on a bunch of grapes.

In the late eighteenth century the Lion had become an important social centre in the town, boasting a fine Adam-style assembly room (see p 125) now decorated in rather brighter colours than it would have borne originally. It has a saucer dome, a minstrel gallery, two carved fireplaces, two large wall mirrors and painted panels with figures on doors and gallery. Here, in 1802, de Quincey slept when travelling to London.

Robert Lawrence who owned the Lion at this period was one of the leading citizens of Shrewsbury and a tablet in St Julian's Church refers to his 'unrelenting exertions, for upwards of thirty years, in opening the great road through Wales between the United Kingdoms, as also for establishing the first mail-coach to this town'. Lawrence died in 1806, two years after Prince William Frederick (afterwards William IV) had stayed for four days at the Lion and attended a ball in the assembly room.

In the 1820s Jack Mytton, the Shropshire hunting squire, often came to the inn for port. 'Nimrod' describes one of these visits:[32]

> On going into the bar one evening when somewhat 'sprung' by wine, he was told there was a box in the coach office for him, which contained two brace of foxes. He requested it to be brought to him; then taking up a poker, he knocked off the lid with it, and let the foxes out in the room in which the landlady and some of her female friends were assembled—giving a thrilling view-holloa at the time. Now it cannot be said they 'broke cover' in good style; but it may be safely asserted that they broke such a great quantity of bottles, glasses and crockery ware, as to have rendered the joke an expensive one.

In 1830 Madame Tussaud held an exhibition of waxworks in the Lion assembly room which was lit throughout with coloured lights and in August 1831 Nicolo Paganini, the great violinist, played in the same room before his departure to the Court of St Petersburg. Jenny Lind, the Swedish soprano, sang in the assembly room on several occasions.

In 1836 Charles Dickens stayed at the Lion with his illustrator Hablot Browne and used the hotel again twenty years later on one of his provincial reading tours.

During the General Election of June 1841, Benjamin Disraeli, who was staying at the Lion, wrote on the hotel notepaper to the Prime Minister, Sir Robert Peel, as the results were coming in. In the letter, which hangs in the hall of the hotel, he says: 'The State of the Poll at Shrewsbury this day permits me to renew my fealty to my chief.'

For over a hundred years the Lion was a famous coaching inn though the hilly approach presented difficulty to all but the most experienced drivers. Hayward, one of the old coach drivers was

> . . . accustomed to come up the hill at full gallop, pull his four horses round at top speed and dash through the opening with only inches to spare. He did this every day for many years, and never had an accident. When we consider the extreme difficulty of handling four horses and a lumbering coach this exploit seems little short of miraculous.[33]

SOUTHAMPTON, Hampshire

The Dolphin in the High Street dates back to the fifteenth century. There was a property called 'le Dolphyn' on the site in 1454 but the first reference to the premises as an inn was in 1548. The landlord at this time was Edward Wilmott who later became the mayor and also Member of Parliament for Southampton. Very little of this sixteenth-century building remains. The half-timbered archway to the yard is Tudor, there are early stone-mullioned windows in the left wing and the cellars are also early. It was at this first inn that Sir Humphrey Gilbert dined in 1582 when planning England's first colonies in the New World.

The Dolphin became important as a meeting place in the early part of the seventeenth century. In 1635 Archbishop Laud met in the inn with the ecclesiastical commissioners to report on the churchgoing habits of the Puritan community. In the same period the Mayor and Corporation of Southampton entertained the Ambassador of the King of Morocco at the Dolphin. In 1648, John Taylor, 'the Water Poet', mentioned the inn as a resting place on the three day journey from London to Carisbrook in the Isle of Wight where Charles I was then imprisoned. He wrote of the horses:

With firey speed the foaming bit they champt on
And brought us to the Dolphin at Southampton.

In 1760, or thereabouts, there was considerable rebuilding and the present Georgian brick façade was added with its remarkable large bow windows on the upper floors (see p 125). The ground floor, which has a coaching entrance, is rusticated. Above the entrance is a balcony. At this time Southampton was a fashionable centre and the Dolphin shared in the prosperity brought by coaching traffic, the sea commerce, and society.

Edward Gibbon, who served as a captain in the Hampshire militia from 1759 to 1770, often visited the Dolphin where, in 1762, he entertained the City Fathers on the occasion when he was made a Burgess of Southampton.

The assembly room was used as a ballroom from 1785: Jane Austen was a subscriber to the balls and attended with her mother and sister Cassandra, in 1808. She went as often as possible 'to have a good bargain'.

The façade of the Dolphin carries the arms of William IV and Queen Adelaide, indicating royal approval granted in the 1830s. William Makepeace Thackeray was greatly attracted to the Dolphin where he wrote part of *Pendennis* (1848-50). Many years later Queen Victoria stayed at the hotel and the stables were used for her horses when travelling from London to Osborne House in the Isle of Wight. It was quite an entourage. In 1898 the local paper reported:

> . . . the Queen's private carriage with two others, and eleven horses and ten servants arrived at Southampton . . . and proceeded to the Dolphin Hotel where she will stay the night.

During World War I, Field Marshal Earl Haig (then General Haig) used the Dolphin as his headquarters when preparing in 1914 for the embarkation of the British Expeditionary Force for France. The round table he used for his conference is still among the furnishings.

The Duke of Wellington in Bugle Street is on the site of a twelfth-century stone house (the foundations and cellars of which still remain) and was, from 1220, owned by Benedict Ace, one of the earliest named mayors of Southampton (1237-45). When the French raided the city in 1338 the house was damaged and afterwards had to be partly rebuilt. It was incorporated c1490 into the inn by a brewer, Rowland Johnson, and was named Bere House. It has remained an inn ever since but the name was changed to the Duke of Wellington soon after the Battle of Waterloo.

The present building of three storeys, timber-framed and gabled, with the upper storeys overhanging, was damaged by enemy action in World War II and was restored under the supervision of a local architect, Bernard H. Dale, in 1962-3.

The Red Lion in the High Street is near to the Royal Pier. The cellar dates back to the twelfth century but the main building, though altered and restored, is of Tudor origin. The inn is noted for Henry V's Court Room, a half-timbered hall with a fine Tudor fireplace and a gallery (see p 126), probably used in medieval times by the trade guilds for their meetings and banquets. Such a hall would have been an appropriate place to choose for the hastily arranged treason trial which took place there on 2 August 1415. Richard, Earl of Cambridge, Lord Scrope of Masham, and Sir Thomas Grey of Heton were accused of conspiracy against the life and crown of Henry V. The king was in Southampton preparing his army for the invasion of France which was to result in the capture of Harfleur and Agincourt. He summoned a jury and the three conspirators were found guilty, condemned to death, and executed outside the Bargate nearby. A rubbing from a stone describing the execution is framed in the court room and the coats of arms of the noblemen who officiated at the trial can be seen on the walls. They were the Duke of York, Baron Camoys, the Duke of Bedford, the Earl of Warwick, the Duke of Exeter and the Earl of Westmorland. There is also an early militia flag bearing the coat of arms granted to Southampton by Queen Elizabeth in 1575.

The façade of the Red Lion is not impressive, but no one should be deterred by this from entering the court room. The trial held there is the subject of Shakespeare's *King Henry V*, Act II, Scene II.

The Star, close to the Dolphin on the same side of the High Street, has vaulted cellars which probably date from medieval times when there was a house on the site. Evidence from old documents points to the possibility that there was an inn here in 1601 but most of the present building is Georgian. In the eighteenth century the inn was a coaching terminus and social centre. It has four storeys surmounted by a balustraded parapet bearing the royal arms in gilt and colour. A long white-and-gold balcony spans the whole frontage at first floor level and above this is a gilded lettered sign. The ground floor which is rusticated has a central yard entrance bearing the following words:

COACH TO LONDON
(Sundays excepted)
Alresford Alton
Performs 10 hours.

In 1831 the Duchess of Kent with Princess Victoria, then twelve years of age, stayed in the hotel for three days. A Victoria Room commemorates the visit.

SOUTHWELL, Nottinghamshire

The Saracen's Head, formerly the King's Arms, is an old timber-framed inn now fronted with stucco. The second storey overhangs slightly and there is a slate roof but its age is revealed in the timbered entrance to the yard with its heavy wooden gates. The inn has been used by kings and nobles since the twelfth century. The dates when royal visitors have been entertained are listed in the hall:

1194 Richard I
1213 King John
1223 and 1258 Henry III
1281 Edward I
1331 Edward III
1395, 1396 and 1398 Richard II
1646 Charles I.

It was on 5 May 1646 at Southwell that Charles I gave himself into the hands of the Scottish Commissioners who handed him over to the Parliamentarians for £400,000. He never regained his freedom and was beheaded in Whitehall on 30 January 1649.

In the nineteenth century the Saracen's Head was a posting house and housed the Inland Revenue Office.

SOUTH ZEAL, Devon

The Oxenham Arms in this village, 4 miles east of Okehampton, is mentioned in Charles Kingsley's *Westward Ho!* (1855). At one time it was the manor house of the Burgoyne family and before that may have been part of a twelfth-century monastery. The present building is sixteenth or early seventeenth century, solidly built of granite and oak beams, with fine stone work fireplaces.

The inn was well known to the author and playwright, Eden Phillpotts, who describes it as 'the stateliest and most ancient abode in the hamlet'.

SPALDING, Lincolnshire

The White Hart in the Market Place serves what Lord Torrington in 1790 called a 'Dutch-like canal town', now the centre of the Fenland bulb-growing industry. The inn dates from 1377, hence the white hart of Richard II. Tradition has it that it was the priory guesthouse and that Chaucer stayed here on his visits to the priory. It was rebuilt early in the sixteenth century and Tudor work includes moulded beams in the wings that enclose the yard. A fire in 1714 made it necessary to rebuild some parts and the frontage is even later. Bombing during the World War II made further restoration necessary.

In 1586 Mary Queen of Scots is said to have spent a night in the Crown Room of the inn on her way to Fotheringhay. After the Civil War, Robert Rishton, one of Cromwell's 'Ironsides' became the landlord and in 1666 he issued trade tokens which bore a hart couchant on one side and a lion rampant on the other.

STAFFORD

The Swan is an eighteenth-century coaching inn which may have been built on the site of an earlier inn of 1440. It carries a plaque which refers to its association with George Borrow and his *Romany Rye* (1857). Borrow clearly loved this inn. He came here after parting from Isopel Berners in Mumpers Dingle and found it a place of infinite life and bustle:

> Travellers of all descriptions, from all the cardinal points, were continually stopping at it. Jacks creaked in the kitchens, turning round spits on which large joints of meat piped and smoked before great fires. There was running up and down the stairs, and along galleries, slamming of doors, cries of 'Coming, Sir' and 'Please-to-step-this-way, ma'am' during 18 hours of the four and twenty.

Borrow's feeling for the Swan was such that he wrote that often in later life, when lonely and melancholy, he recalled the time he spent there and 'never failed to become cheerful from the recollection'.

Charles Dickens who once stayed in the Swan was less enthusiastic and called it 'the extinct town inn, the Dodo'.

STAMFORD, Lincolnshire

The George lies on the old Great North Road through Stamford which is now bypassed. This beautiful limestone building is one of nearly 450 buildings in this small town scheduled as 'of architectural and historic interest'. The George announces its presence in a fine gallows sign which spans the road well clear of all 'high loads'.

Parts of the building date back to the eleventh century when it was a hospice used by the Knights of St John of Jerusalem The crypt certainly belongs to this period but it is difficult to distinguish the medieval parts from those in which medieval fragments have been used during rebuilding. The cloakrooms on the ground floor have a special interest. The ladies powder room has a thirteenth-century chamfered pointed arch; the gentleman's toilet is part of a medieval kitchen with a passage of timber-framed screens and a large fireplace. This was originally part of an old house known as the Hermitage, added to enlarge the hotel. Other medieval features are recorded in the first report of the Stamford Survey Group.[34]

The main block was built in 1597 by Lord Burghley, Lord High Treasurer to Queen Elizabeth I. The centre of the building contains an old chimney stack to be seen in the lounge. The stone fireplace and what appears to be an old bread oven, the whole surmounted by two enormous beams, was uncovered some years ago when a plastered wall was demolished.

A stone arch of this period may be seen to the left of the frontage of the inn which is eighteenth-century rebuilding. During this period and well into the nineteenth century the George became an important coaching inn roughly half way between London and Edinburgh. Passengers waited for the coaches in the beautifully panelled London Room to the left of the present entrance, once the approach to the courtyard.

Many famous guests have used the George including Charles I in 1645, the Duke of Cumberland in 1745 as he returned from the victory at Culloden, and Sir Walter Scott on one of his journeys from London to Scotland.

In the entrance hall to the hotel there is a painting of Daniel Lambert, the son of the Keeper of Leicester Prison who, in 1789, when nineteen years of age, started to gain weight very rapidly, despite the fact that he ate moderately and drank only water. Moreover he was an active youth and loved sports, particularly coursing and fishing. Eventually he turned his disability to account and started to tour to exhibit his corpulence. He was on tour and seemingly in good health despite his weight of 52 stone 11lb when he died in Stamford at the age of 39. His enormous walking stick lies below his portrait in the George.

In the nineteenth century the George was the main Tory centre in the town and the **Stamford Hotel,** built in 1810 with the help and approval of Lord Gainsborough, was the main centre for the Whig party. This is a large building with a pillared façade. It carries a sculpture of 'Justice' by J. C. F. Rossi, RA, then sculptor to the Prince of Wales.

STOCKBRIDGE, Hampshire

The Grosvenor, formerly the King's Head, is an early nineteenth-century yellow-brick three-storey building with a large central pillared portico supporting a room on the first floor. It was once owned by Tom Cannon, the jockey and trainer, and in its early days was much used by the racing fraternity. Since then it has been a resort of fishermen who frequent the River Test. It is the headquarters of the exclusive Houghton Club, formed in 1822, which is restricted to twenty-two members. The club room contains the stuffed remains of some of the largest fish to have been caught in the river.

STRATFORD-UPON-AVON, Warwickshire

The Falcon is close to the Guild Chapel and the Grammar School, both old buildings which must have been very familiar to Shakespeare. He would have known the Falcon as a private house for it did not become an inn until 1640. It is a half-timbered building of three storeys set on a stonework foundation, with close set uprights and horizontal timbers at the floor levels. There are lattice windows on all floors, those on the ground floor built out as canted bays. Until 1930 the timbering was plastered over.

The most notable innkeeper of the Falcon was Joseph Phillips who appears to have been in charge from about 1640. They were obviously prosperous years for he supplied wine to the town and issued his own trade tokens.

The Shakespeare Club was founded in the Falcon in 1824.

The Red Horse in Bridge Street embraces an earlier inn known as The Golden Lion and, before 1623, as The Peacocke Inn. It contains the armchair and poker used by Washington Irving who, writing as Geoffrey Crayon, gave us a description of the little parlour:

> . . . to a homeless man, there is a momentary feeling of something like independence when, after a weary day's travel he stretches himself before an inn fire ; . . . the arm chair is his throne, the poker his sceptre, and the little parlour his undisputed empire.

No doubt he also enjoyed being led to his room by Hannah Cuppage, the pretty maid who escorted him bearing a candle. It was in the Red Horse parlour that he wrote *The Sketch Book* (1819).

Prince Rupert slept in the Red Horse in 1643 and it later became a house much frequented by actors including Thomas Betterton, Charles Macklin and David Garrick.

The Shakespeare in Chapel Street has nine timbered gables which form the third storey of a half-timbered building with close-set uprights. The gabled storey overhangs. Part of the inn may originally have been the Great House of Sir Hugh Clopton (d1496) which existed in Shakespeare's day. The other part was a building known as the Five Gables. It is not known when the premises were first licensed. It may not have become an inn until the eighteenth century when, like the Red Horse, it was used by actors.

The White Swan in Rother Street may have started as the house of a wealthy Stratford merchant c1450 but it has been an inn since Shakespeare's time when it was known as The King's Head. The ancient features are inside the building. Until 1927 the living room walls of the old house were covered with Jacobean panelling. In that year the panelling was removed revealing on the plaster early paintings dating from between 1555 and 1565. They depict the story of Tobit from the Apocrypha but the figures are in sixteenth-century costume (see p 143).

The inn has black timbers, fine panelling and a carved Jacobean mantelpiece. In a first floor bedroom, originally the Solar where the master of the house lodged, is a fine king-post roof and a small stone window of Gothic design which, when it was first put in place, must have looked out over the Forest of Arden.

During World War II the White Swan was an American Red Cross Centre.

STRETTON, Rutland

The Ram Jam, on the Great North Road between Stamford and Grantham, is a stone building constructed around a fourteenth-century alehouse which was thatched. A sketch by

Samuel Hieronymus Grimm in the British Museum shows the thatched alehouse as it was in the seventeenth century. There is a copy on the wall of the bar which is the only remaining part of the original alehouse. A massive beam over the fireplace has been carbon dated and is said to be over 1,000 years old.

The name Ram Jam is unique. The story goes that a friendly passenger from one of the passing coaches promised to divulge a secret to the landlord and his wife. He asserted that he could draw both mild and bitter beer from the same barrel. When the landlord had left for a while, the visitor demonstrated to his wife how the trick could be done. He made a hole in one side of the barrel and told her to ram her thumb into it. Then he made a second hole on the other side and told her to jam her other thumb against that. Having immobilised her, he told her to hang on while he fetched the pegs for the holes. He did not return but left her there and departed without paying his bill. The incident is commemorated in the inn sign.

There is an alternative explanation for the name. In 1740 an army sergeant, recently returned from India, became the landlord of the inn. He produced a unique liquor which he sold in small flasks under the name of Ram Jam which he said was the Indian name for 'table servant'.

The Ram Jam inn is associated with the second of two famous fights between Tom Cribb, Champion of England, and Tom Molyneaux, an American negro. Molyneaux slept in the inn and the fight took place at Thirlestone Gap in Leicestershire, about 3½ miles away, on 28 September 1811. In an earlier fight at East Grinstead on 18 December 1810, Molyneaux had pinioned Cribb so that he could not fall or hit. The crowd was infuriated and tore him away from his opponent. Cribb was nearly beaten when he failed to answer the call of 'time' but one of his seconds accused Molyneaux of having bullets in his hand and the delay gave Cribb time to recover. Cribb won the fight but his victory was disputed and a second contest was arranged to take place in Leicestershire. For this fight Cribb was trained by a Captain Barclay and he beat Molyneaux who suffered a broken jaw after eight rounds.

The inn has two contemporary coloured prints of the fight. One was published by Walker & Knight of Cornhill on 3 October 1811 and the other by Thomas Tegg of Cheapside on 16 October. To produce a print in five days at a time when news was carried by mail coach and the work had to be done by a hand engraver was a remarkable achievement.

The façade of the Ram Jam carries an old Saxon sundial unearthed when the present inn was built.

STROOD, Kent

The Crispin and Crispianus is a two-storey brick-built inn which has a weather-boarded upper storey which overhangs. Crispin and Crispianus were Roman brothers who fled to Gaul during the persecution of the Christians by Emperor Diocletian. They settled to make a living as shoemakers but were martyred at Soissons in AD 308. St Crispin is the patron saint of shoemakers. The inn is said by some to have been founded by a soldier who returned from Agincourt, a battle fought on 25 October 1415—St Crispin's Day. The link is referred to in Shakespeare's Henry V:

> And Crispin, Crispian shall n'er go by
> From this day to the ending of the world,
> But we in it shall be remembered . . .

It is much more likely to have been the meeting place for the local guild of shoemakers. The guilds often met in taverns. As the old proverb says—'cobblers and tinkers are the best ale drinkers'.

Charley Roberts, a man who had been an ostler in the coaching inns of Rochester, was once lodged at the inn out of charity. A widower, he made a living by selling lace, thread and tape and on Sundays shaved local labourers. On 20 September 1830 he was taken seriously ill and when the doctor came to see the dying man, Roberts revealed the fact that his real name was Charles Parrott Hanger, and that he was a nephew of Colonel George Hanger who had been a close friend of the Prince Regent at Brighton. He asked the doctor to act as his executor and it was found that this apparently destitute man had left £1,000 to a son, Charles Henry Hanger, in Birmingham.[35]

Charles Dickens often visited the Crispin and Crispianus when he was at Gad's Hill Place. It is mentioned in the paper on 'Tramps' in *The Uncommercial Traveller.*

TAN HILL, Yorkshire

Tan Hill Inn in the remote Arkengarthdale valley, 11 miles north-east of Reeth in Swaledale, and 4½ miles from the nearest village of Keld, is 1,732ft above sea level, the highest licensed house in England. (Tan is the Celtic word for fire or beacon.) The inn is basically a stone cottage with a grey slate roof and a large projecting porch which shelters the entrance from strong winds. It remains much as it was when first built as a resthouse for the Tan Hill coal miners and carters who lived in 'bothies' during the week, returning to their homes only at weekends. It was used by farmers fetching coal from the mines and by pedlars travelling between Yorkshire and Northumberland. The miners enjoyed their sports on Tan Hill including hound trails and 'bruising'—fighting with bare fists.[36]

TEWKESBURY, Gloucestershire

The Bell is an Elizabethan building close to the River Avon and the Abbey Mill. It may well have started as a monastic hospice in the thirteenth century; wall paintings of this period have been found on interior walls. The inn is half-timbered with three storeys and three gables, the upper storeys with a slight overhang. There is a timber porch, and above it hangs a bell-sign on a bracket. The initials and date—I K 1696—on the façade are said to be associated with a restoration of the building.

The Bell Inn was used in *John Halifax, Gentleman* (1857), the novel by Mrs Craik whose maiden name was Dinah Maria Mulock. She first visited Tewkesbury in 1852 and was so impressed with the town that she decided to make it the scene of her fourth book. On a later visit she took a meal at the Bell Inn where she learnt that it had once been the house of a tanner. This was chosen as the trade of Abel Fletcher, the Quaker mill-owner who became the hero of her story which was mainly written while she was staying at Amberley in the Cotswolds. Mrs Craik visited the Bell again shortly before she died in 1887.

The Hop Pole is best known as an old coaching inn, the hostelry where Mr Pickwick with his party—Ben Allen, Bob Sawyer and Sam Weller—stopped to dine. The visit is described in *The Pickwick Papers* (1836-7):

> Upon which occasion, we are assured, there was more bottled ale, with some more Madeira, and some port besides; and here the case-bottle was replenished for the fourth time. Under the influence of these combined stimulants, Mr Pickwick and Mr Ben Allen fell asleep for thirty miles, while Bob Sawyer and Sam Weller sang duets in the dickey.

The three-storey Queen Anne inn is built on to an adjoining half-timbered building with dormer windows. At one time a central archway led to the back of the inn; today an impressive Victorian porch supported by iron pillars spans the pavement outside and provides the main entrance. This is surmounted by some intricate ironwork and by the royal arms. A gilded lettered sign spans the main frontage at third-floor level. The walls are white; the windows, cornice and entrance are painted black.

THAME, Oxfordshire

The Spread Eagle is an old red-brick coaching inn noted for its magnificent wrought-iron sign. This formerly hung from the inn as a bracket sign but when John Fothergill became the landlord in 1922 part of the wall holding the sign was beginning to crumble. He decided to convert the sign into a post sign. The ironwork had been made in 1834 by a blacksmith of Long Crendon called Timms. In 1924 this was adjusted by Ralph Timms, his grandson, the sign was painted by 'Carrington' Partridge, and the lettering was done by Spencer Hoffman.[37]

THAMES DITTON, Surrey

The Swan is a black and white Thames-side inn of two storeys with a terrace overlooking the water. In 1834 Theodore Hook wrote this poem in a punt on the river:

> The 'Swan' snug inn, good fare affords
> At table e'er was put on,
> And worthier quite of loftier boards
> It's poultry, fish and mutton.
>
> And while sound wine mine host supplies,
> With beer of Meux or Tritton,
> Mine hostess, with her bright blue eyes,
> Invites to stay at Ditton

At about the same time William Hone's *Table Book* praised the landlord's wife (possibly the same lady) but as a cook:

> The Swan Inn . . . remarkable for the neatness and comfort of its appearance, and for the still more substantial attraction of its internal accommodation, is kept by Mr. John Lock, a most civil, good-natured and obliging creature; . . . he has a wife absolutely incomparable in the preparation of 'stewed ells' and not to be despised in the art of cooking a good beef-steak, or a mutton chop.

THETFORD, Norfolk

The Bell in King Street was founded in 1493 when it was the property of the College of the Virgin Mary in Thetford. It is timbered with close-set uprights on the ground floor. The upper floor overhangs and there are tall brick chimneys (see p 143). A massive timber corner post where the London Road meets King Street was at one time the official place for posting public proclamations and many old nails used for this purpose can still be seen embedded in the wood. On the northern side of the courtyard there was once an open gallery at first-floor level, but this has been enclosed by an outer wall. It can, however, be traced inside the inn where it now forms a corridor to some bedrooms in which traces of the old wattle and daub construction of the original wall may still be seen. There are also Elizabethan wall paintings to be seen in some of the bedrooms, discovered when layers of wallpaper and textile fabric were removed.

The Bell was an important coaching and posting house in the eighteenth century. An announcement by a landlord, Thomas Feltwell, who took over the inn in 1753, proudly stated in the *Ipswich Journal*:

> The Bell Inn was, and is, the Post-House; there are close Post Chaises with Steel Springs, and very able horses; the Excise Office is kept there; The Norwich Stage coaches now inn there . . . also the Cambridge Carrier to and from Norwich.

THIRSK, Yorkshire

The Golden Fleece overlooking the cobbled Market Place dates mainly from the early eighteenth century though it certainly existed in earlier times. The older part is of three storeys, brick-built with a central entrance and later bay windows at street level. Above the entrance is a wrought-iron bracket sign from which hangs a golden fleece.

Until 1815 the only coaching inn in Thirsk was the Three Tuns. In 1815, however, the landlady of the Three Tuns, Mrs Alice Cass, retired and handed over her coaching trade to her relative, George Blyth, at the Golden Fleece. At this time the house was a low, two-storey building, about half its present size, but Blyth was able to buy some adjoining property including a tall brick house with arched windows which provided an access to the rear. It then became a great coaching house with stabling for at least sixty horses. Blyth died in 1828 but the trade was carried on by his nephew John Hall and later by John's son, William Hall. Their portraits still hang in the inn and so does the old Parliament clock.

The Golden Fleece has always been a social centre for the local farming community.

TONBRIDGE, Kent

Ye Olde Chequers in the High Street dates from 1270. The present building is mainly sixteenth century but still retains some original timbering. There is a central section of two storeys with dormer windows in the roof, and on either side are gabled wings of three storeys, the upper floors overhanging. The timbered gables have decorative bargeboards. The sign is in the form of a gibbet placed where the original gibbet stood in the fourteenth century when the inn was in the centre of the town overlooking the Market Place and stocks. Wat Tyler's brother is said to have been the last man to have been hanged outside the Chequers.

The Rose and Crown on the opposite side of the High Street was a posting inn in the eighteenth century and by 1835 had become a coaching centre on the road to Tunbridge Wells and Hastings. The earliest record of the inn is dated 1625 and an indenture of 1695 refers to the inn as 'knowne by the name of the sign of the Roase and Crowne'. The present frontage of three storeys, built of chequered red and blue brick, dates from the early eighteenth century (see p 144). There is a fine pillared portico carrying the arms of the Duchess of Kent who came to the hotel with Princess Victoria. The interior still has rooms with old beams and Jacobean panelling.

The Rose and Crown has close associations with the Skinners' Company. Tonbridge School was founded by Sir Andrew Judd in the reign of Edward VI. The school was left by him, in trust, to the Skinners' Company and when Masters, Warden and Court make their annual visit to Tonbridge they meet at the hotel. At one time the Master used Room 17 so that he could make an appearance above the porch to greet an assembly of boys outside but modern traffic problems have made it impossible to continue the custom.

Tom Pawlet who became proprietor in 1893 was a keen cricketer. For nearly fifty years he was secretary of the Tonbridge Cricket Club and did much to establish Tonbridge Cricket week. He played for Kent and at the time of his death in 1923 was manager of the Kent County Cricket Club. Needless to say, many cricketers used the Rose and Crown.

TROUTBECK, Westmorland

The Mortal Man at Troutbeck was first built in 1689 though the present hotel reveals little evidence of its history. The post sign, however, which stands by the roadside, shows two men, one happy and robust holding a foaming mug, the other thin and pale. This is a modern version of the original alehouse sign which was painted by the artist Julius Caesar Ibbotson in the eighteenth century to pay for his stay during a sketching and fishing trip. The original verse carried on the sign was:

O mortal man, that lives by bread,
What is it makes thy face so red?
Thou silly fop that looks so pale,
'Tis drinking Tommy Birkett's ale.

Today's version has replaced 'face' by 'nose', 'fop' by 'fool' and 'Tommy' by 'Sally'.

UPTON-ON-SEVERN, Worcestershire

The White Lion dates from the seventeenth century although it has a later façade in classical style with fluted pilasters and a large pillared porch supporting an effigy of a lion rampant. The interior of the inn was reconstructed in 1971 but some of the early timber construction is still to be seen.

The famous actress, Sarah Siddons, once performed at the White Lion with a group of strolling players. In fiction it is the scene of episodes from Henry Fielding's *The History of Tom Jones* (1749) when he brought 'our hero and his redeemed lady into the famous town of Upton and they went directly to that inn which in their eyes presented the fairest appearance in the street, a house of exceedingly good repute'.

A former landlord of the White Lion has the distinction of figuring in what is perhaps the best known of all epitaphs:

Beneath this stone in hope of Zion
Doth lie the landlord of 'The Lion';
Resigned unto the heavenly will,
His son keeps on the business still.

WANSFORD, Huntingdonshire

The Haycock lies on the southern side of a river-crossing where a stone bridge was built in the reign of Edward III to take the Great North Road across the Nene. The present inn was built as a posting house in 1632 on the site of an earlier inn. A local freestone has been used and the roof, which is of Collyweston slate, is said to cover an area of more than an acre. The stage-coaches originally swung round in front of the inn, passed through the arch that is now the front entrance, and rumbled through the centre of the house to the courtyard. The horses were then tethered in the cooling arch, now the archway to the second yard. The tethering rings are still to be seen on the archway wall. Passengers alighted in the yard and mounted wooden stairways straight to an open gallery surrounding the yard and to the bedrooms. This gallery was enclosed early in the nineteenth century to form a passageway. The old yard could stable 150 horses at one time. The second courtyard contained the brewhouse and the cockfighting loft.

The name 'Haycock' dates back to 1636 when a man called Barnaby visited Wansford where the plague was rife in the village. He lay down to sleep on a haycock. John Taylor, the Water Poet, describes the subsequent event:

> On a haycock sleeping soundly
> The river rose and took me roundly
> Down the current: people cried,
> As along the stream I hied.
> 'Where away?' quoth they 'From Greenland?'
> 'No ; from Wansford Bridge in England'.

Celia Fiennes gives a slightly different version of the story as she heard it in 1698:

> . . . a man makeing hay fell asleep on a heap of it and a great storme washed the hay and the man into the River, and carry'd him to the Bridge, where he awoke and knew not where he was, called to the people in the grounds and told them he lived in a place called Wanstead in England, which goes as a jest on the men of Wanstead to this day.

Another version is that the river was floooded by Collyweston workers to take barges of slate down the river.

The inn carries a painted wall sign of Barnaby on the haycock beneath Wansford bridge.

It is said that Mary Queen of Scots was brought by her jailer, Sir William Fitzwilliam, to the inn on the site of the present

Haycock on her way to imprisonment at Fotheringhay Castle in 1586. Since then the Haycock has had a fascinating history which may be summarised chronologically:

1790 Lord Torrington records a visit to the inn in his diary:

> . . . nothing could equal my good dinner but my good disposition towards it. This is a nice Inn. Everything clean and in order, the beds and stabling excellent.

1804 The Haycock was taken over by a Mr Mallatratt who was 'determined to keep a good larder, with a plentiful supply of tench, pike and other fish'.

1832 The Haycock passed to the Percival family.

1835 On 2 September Princess Alexandrina Victoria and her mother the Duchess of Kent, dined and slept in the Haycock on their way to visit the Archbishop of York at Bishopthorpe Palace.

1870 Fred Archer started his career in the Haycock yard to become a leading jockey and the inn had many visitors from abroad, attracted by the hunting.

1887 Business declined, the licence was surrendered and the property became a farm.

1899 The Haycock became the private residence of Lord Chesham.

1906 Lionel Digby used the Haycock as a racing stable with over 100 horses in training.

1928 Lord Fitzwilliam succeeded in securing a licence for the Haycock again after fighting the case through three courts to the House of Lords.

WANTAGE, Berkshire

The Bear is set back from the Market Square and has a cobbled forecourt in which stands a well-painted post sign. The inn was built in the second half of the eighteenth century and this was its busiest period as a coaching inn. The great gates which led to the cobbled courtyard where the coaches pulled to a halt may still be seen and stone archways in the brick walls of the old yard reveal where the stables used to be. In addition to the post sign, the name is blazoned in gold letters on a blue ground along the parapet; there is an effigy of a bear on the façade and even the stress plates which hold the tie-bars have been cut out in the shape of a bear. In the 1960s, the interior was entirely reconstructed but original outside walls remain.

The Berkshire Downs which lie to the south of Wantage are noted for the training of racehorses and the Bear has always been a natural meeting place for owners and trainers. One day when the trainers were having their annual dinner at the inn they failed to invite the only local lady who owned and trained her own racehorse. In the middle of the dinner she arrived with a lion. The result of the visit is not recorded, but there was certainly some consternation at the table, followed by a lively scene. The lion was, in fact, a tame animal but she had made her point.

WELLS, Somerset

The Crown, on the south side of the Market Place, is a late seventeenth-century timber-framed building with three storeys and three gables. The early work can best be seen in the courtyard where there are five latticed oriel windows with fine carving on the frames and bracket supports. Below the windows on the first floor are wall panels with the fleur-de-lys. An eighteenth-century Wells physician, Claver Morris, records in his diary his regular weekly visits to the Crown Coffee House as it was then called. Here he read the newspapers, met friends, gossiped, transacted business and even saw patients, for it was a common practice in those days for a doctor to attend a coffee house regularly where he could be consulted.

WEST MEON, Hampshire

West Meon Hut, a seventeenth-century coaching inn where the horses were changed on the London to Fareham run, lies about 1½ miles north of West Meon village. It was once known as The George; the Ordnance Survey map still gives both names. When the Meon Valley railway was authorised in 1897, many Irish workers were brought in and a hut was built behind the George and licensed as a drinking place for their use. After the railway was opened in 1903, the name stuck to the premises and has been used to this day. The old inn is strategically situated at the crossing of two major roads—the A32 and the A272.

WHITCHURCH, Hampshire

The White Hart is a crossroads inn built where the old London to Exeter road crossed the road from Oxford to Southampton. In coaching days travellers who had to change coaches were often forced to wait in the inn for considerable periods for their connection. As many as twenty coaches a day called at the White Hart.

Some landlords have claimed that the inn existed in 1461—the year when Edward IV, a keen promoter of wayside inns, came to the throne.

The present building is transitional between the Stuart and Queen Anne styles and was probably built c1700. It is sited on a corner and here the building carries a portico with Ionic pillars, above which stands an effigy sign of a white hart (see p 144). The dining room has a fine plaster ceiling of c1700.

In 1832 the Rev John Henry Newman spent ten hours in the White Hart waiting for the Exeter mail coach on his way from Oxford to Falmouth and was joined by the Rev Richard Hurrell Froude, a leader of the Tractarian movement and brother of the historian. While waiting, Newman is said to have written verses which were later published in *Lyra Apostolica* (1834) including the lines on guardian angels—'Are these the tracks of an unearthly friend?'

Charles Kingsley was a frequent visitor to the White Hart where he stayed when fishing the Test. On 26 May 1863 he wrote of the inn.

> I like this place, and that is the truth. It is old without being decayed. This low room has a beautiful Queen Anne ceiling and could, by withdrawing the partition, be enlarged from the clubroom into the ballroom in which the three belles and one-and-a-half beaux of Whitchurch would have full room to dance.

The inn is mentioned in Kingsley's *Two Years Ago* (1857),

and *The Water Babies* (1863) was influenced by his fishing experiences in this locality.

WIMBORNE MINSTER, Dorset

The King's Head overlooking the Square, was first mentioned in 1726 when it was a two-storey red-brick building with bow windows. In 1848 it was described as a 'Family Hotel, Commercial Inn and Posting House', at a period when it was run by Thomas Laing who used to ride to the local hounds and entertained the hunt in the Square with 'Brown Brandy' for which his house was noted. In 1889 the owner, William Ellis, rebuilt the hotel. He added a storey, removed the bow windows, plastered the frontage to resemble stone and built a heavy porch with a balcony above from which poll declarations have since been made at parliamentary elections. At the same time he built the Victoria Hall next door which was used for many years on market days as a corn exchange and at other times as a hall for concerts, plays and dances. It later became a cinema and in 1930 was converted to become part of the hotel to provide a dining room and kitchen, with ballroom above.

The painted sign shows King Henry VII whose mother founded Wimborne Grammar School.

WINCHESTER, Hampshire

The Eclipse faces Winchester Cathedral in the Close and is approached through the narrow entrance from the High Street known as the Pentice. On the left of the Pentice is the Church of St Lawrence built upon the site of the Chapel Royal of the Palace of William the Conqueror. The rector of St Lawrence had a rectory which backed on to the church and this is now the Eclipse inn, a pre-reformation timbered building, probably fourteenth century, which has been well restored. The spandrels of the Tudor-style timber door frame have small painted signs of the earth, moon and sun 'in eclipse'. In the 1930s it was, for a time, a tea house.

The name of the inn comes from the famous Derby winner Eclipse, a horse bred by the Duke of Northumberland and born during the eclipse of 1763. Eclipse was never defeated.

Major O'Kelly, his owner, used to say 'Eclipse first, the rest nowhere'.

The Royal Hotel in St Peter Street also has ecclesiastical origins. It was built as a private house in the seventeenth century as part of the Roman Catholic settlement established by Roger Corham and was known as Bishop's House. In 1794 a group of nuns fled from Brussels to England when religious persecution was spreading in Europe after the French Revolution. They were given the Bishop's House which became a nunnery for over fifty years. In 1857 the convent moved to East Bergholt in Suffolk and the house was acquired by C. W. Benny who for some years had run a hostelry called the White Hart near the Town Clock in the High Street. He called the new hotel The Royal and it soon became a social centre in the city.

WINDSOR, Berkshire

The Castle in the High Street of this royal borough is opposite to the Guildhall and close to Windsor Castle and Windsor Great Park. In 1563 it was kept by Agnes Archer and was known as The Bell. By 1721 it had become The Bell and Castle and officially retained that name at least until 1824. The present building was erected as a posting house in the reign of George III with four storeys and an iron balcony at first-floor level. The ground floor walls are rusticated and a gilded lettered sign proclaims its name on the façade. An early reference to this building is contained in a report of 1778 when the third Duke of St Albans sold the furniture of Nell Gwynn's old house and 'Nell's bed was bought by the landlord of the Castle Inn'. The finest rooms in the hotel are those which were added when an adjoining private house was incorporated; a number of them have good plasterwork of the period.

The hotel has had hundreds of notable visitors including privy councillors and others arriving for audiences at the castle. In 1814 the Duke of Wellington was entertained at the hotel when he received the freedom of the borough.

The Old House Hotel on the banks of the Thames by the bridge which separates Windsor and Eton was built in 1676 by Sir Christopher Wren and was used as his private residence when he was comptroller of the works at Windsor Castle. It is a two-storey brick building with a prominent central pediment.

WINGHAM, Kent

The Red Lion and **The Dog Inn** in Wingham date back to 1286 when they formed part of an ecclesiastical building known as Wingham College, a building for a rector and six canons. A fire broke out c1650 and destroyed most of the building on the site of what is now the Dog Inn. This was rebuilt c1661.

The Red Lion building escaped the fire. It has two storeys, the upper storey overhanging. The hipped roof is broken by a small gable above an oriel window over the main entrance. The diamond panes in this window are set in an iron framework and include some very early red glass. The inn is heavily timbered inside and in the private quarters on the upper floor is a small sessions room where the magistrates' Court was held from 1703 until 1886. It has a fine tie-beam and kingpost. The old retiring room used by the magistrates is now a bedroom. A Queen Anne staircase leads to this floor.

In the main lounge is an old minute book of: 'Her Majesty's Justices of the Peace and Commissioners for Taxes. Monthly and Especial Meetings held at the "Redd Lyon" and "Dogg" inns, Wingham, 1703-1712.'

The front entrance to the Red Lion is approached by steps with old iron railings in which the uprights are terminated by acorn finials. Both inns have gibbet signs.

WINTERSLOW, Wiltshire

The Pheasant lies on the A30 about a mile from Winterslow village and 5 miles from Salisbury. It was formerly known as Winterslow Hut. At first sight this clean white building reveals little sign of age. The sign—a large pheasant painted on the eastern gable end—is signed and dated C. Lane 1968. In the eighteenth and the early nineteenth centuries it was a busy coaching inn on what was, and still is, a lonely stretch of road. The Exeter mail coach stopped before proceeding to Salisbury. Thomas Boulter, the Wiltshire highwayman, once held up the mail single-handed close by the Winterslow Hut and took valuables from its passengers.

On 26 October 1816, as the Exeter to London mail coach 'Quicksilver' drew in to the Winterslow Hut, one of the horses was attacked by a lioness which had broken loose from a travelling menagerie bound for Salisbury Fair. A large mastiff sprang to seize the lioness who turned away from the horse, caught the dog and killed it. Eventually a keeper arrived from the menagerie and trapped the lioness. The full account from a contemporary local paper hangs in the hall of the inn together with a print of the scene after James Pollard.

Winterslow has close associations with the critic and essayist William Hazlitt. In 1808 he married and went to live with his wife in a cottage she had inherited in the village. Four years later they moved to London where Hazlitt became the parliamentary reporter, and later the dramatic critic, for the *Morning Chronicle*. In 1819 he left the paper and at about the same time his wife, after a quarrel. He returned to Winterslow and lived in the Winterslow Hut where he did some of his best writing. He was visited here by friends, including Charles and Mary Lamb. Hazlitt describes this as a particularly happy period in his life which tended to be stormy because of his quarrelsome temperament. A portrait of Hazlitt hangs in the bar.

John Forster in his *Life of Charles Dickens* (1872-4) writes of a ride over Salisbury Plain in 1848 with Dickens, John Leech and Mark Lemon 'visiting Stonehenge, and exploring Hazlitt's "hut" at Winterslow, birthplace of some of his finest essays.'

WOKINGHAM, Berkshire

The Old Rose or, as it is now called **Ye Olde Rose Inne,** is not particularly attractive when seen from the Market Place. It is mainly Georgian with Victorian and later additions and the early windows have been fitted with fussy latticed sash windows. It is said that the original frontage was partially destroyed in an election riot. Inside the inn, however, its fifteenth-century origin is revealed in heavy oak beams, panelled rooms and fine stone fireplaces. Early in the eighteenth century four poets who were close friends met in the Old Rose one rainy afternoon. They were John Arbuthnot, John Gay, Alexander Pope and Jonathan Swift. They spent the time composing a twelve verse ballad to the attractive Molly Mog, the landlord's daughter who was being courted by the young squire of Arborfield. In fact she never married but lived to the age of seventy. These are the first two and the last two verses:

The Schoolboy's desire is a play day;
The Schoolmaster's joy is to flog;
The Milkmaid's delight is a May Day,
But mine is on sweet Molly Mog.

Will-a-Wisp leads the traveller gadding
Through ditch and through quagmire and bog;
But no light could set me a-madding
Like the eyes of my sweet Molly Mog.

Were Virgil alive with his Phyllis,
And writing another Eclogue
Both his Phyllis and fair Amaryllis
He'd give up for sweet Molly Mog.

When she smiles on each guest like her liquor
Then jealousy sets me agog,
To be sure, she's a bit for the Vicar
And so I shall lose Molly Mog.

WONERSH, Surrey

The Grantley Arms in this village near Guildford is an old half-timbered manor house with lattice windows, built in the fifteenth century, to which an annexe has been added. It was named after Baron Grantley of Markenfield, previously Fletcher Norton, lawyer, who was elected Tory member of Parliament for Guildford in 1768. He became Attorney General and Speaker of the House of Commons. He was a courageous man who was not afraid to speak his mind even when his views were in direct opposition to those of George III. Because of his forthright speeches he was given the Freedom of the City of London.

YORK, North Riding of Yorkshire

The Black Swan in Peasholme Green is a timber-framed building with two main gables carrying carved bargeboards. The upper storeys overhang.

The building was originally a private house, the home of Wiliam Bowes, MP, Lord Mayor of York in 1417, and of his son William Bowes, Lord Mayor of York in 1443, whose grandson, Sir Martin Bowes was Lord Mayor of London in 1545 and Treasurer of the Mint in the reign of Queen Elizabeth. Sir Martin presented to the City of York the Sword of State which is still borne before the Lord Mayor on the occasion of the monthly meeting in the Guildhall. In 1683 the Black Swan became the home of Edward Thompson, MP, Lord Mayor of York in 1683 and of his daughter, Henrietta Wolfe and her husband, parents of General James Wolfe of Quebec who lived in the house as a child from 1724 to 1726. Subsequently the house became an inn and although much restored it retains its original character and a room on the first floor has some medieval painted panels and a fireplace with Delft tiles.

References

1 Christy, M. *Alfriston and its Star Inn* (1928)
2 Woodruff, D. *The Tichborne Claimant: A Victorian Mystery* (1957)
3 See Hart, G. 'Alexander Pope and the Angel Inn, Andover', *Genealogist's Magazine* (December 1928)
4 Earney, H. W. *Inns of Andover* (third ed, 1971)
5 Boswell, J. *Life of Doctor Johnson* (1791)
6 D'Elboux, R. H. *Pilgrim's Rest* (1955)
7 Oliver, B. *The Renaissance of the English Public House* (1947), 151
8 See *The Taunton Courier*, 3 February 1825
9 See Sitwell, O. and Barton, M. *Brighton* (1935), Ch 1
10 Montagu of Beaulieu, Lord, *Bucklers Hard and its Ships* (1909)
11 Ollard, R. *The Escape of Charles II* (1966)
12 Matz, B. W. *The Inns and Taverns of Pickwick* (1921), photograph facing p 76
13 Daniel, G. *The Ostrich Inn, Colnbrook, Bucks. Its Place in History* (1969)
14 See Deloney, T. *Thomas of Reading* (1632)
15 See Cunningham, A. *Lives of the Most Eminent Painters, Sculptors and Architects* (1833)
16 Hart, C. E. *The Verderers' Court and Speech Court of the Forest of Dean* (Gloucester, 1950)
17 See Richardson, A. E. and Eberlein, H. D. *The English Inn: Past and Present* (1925), fig 57
18 See Williamson, G. C. *The Ancient Crypts in the High Street, Guildford* (1904)

19 Hine, R. L. *The Story of the Sun Hotel, Hitchin* (Hitchin, 1946)
20 Harper, G. C. *Old Inns of Old England* Vol 2 (1906), 45
21 Arrowsmith, R. S. *A Short Historical Sketch of the Parish of Hurstbourne Tarrant* (1907)
22 Sowerby, R. R. *Historical Kirkby Stephen and North Westmorland* (1950), 106
23 Oman, C. *Nelson* (1947), 604
24 Quoted in Thacker, F. S. *General History of the Thames Highway* (1914)
25 Popham, H. E. *The Taverns in the Town* (1937), 69-73
26 Quoted in Watson, R. *A Scrapbook of Inns* (1899)
27 Parker, W. *A History of Long Melford* (1873)
28 Fothergill, J. *Confessions of an Innkeeper* (1938)
29 Pevsner, N. *North Somerset and Bristol* (1958)
30 Jones, W. H. *The Maid's Head Hotel, Norwich: Its Historical Associations* (Norwich, 1947)
31 See Ollard, R. *The Escape of Charles II* (1966) 94-105
32 See Nimrod. *Memoirs of the Life of the Late John Mytton Esq* (1837)
33 Long, G. *English Inns and Roadhouses* (1937), 213
34 Rogers, A. *The Medieval Buildings of Stamford* (Stamford 1970)
35 Harper, G. C. *The Dover Road* (1895)
36 Pontefract, E. *Swaledale* (1934) 55-6
37 Fothergill, J. *My Three Inns* (1949) 19-20

General Bibliography

Aldin, C. *Old Inns* (1921)
Askwith, Lord. *British Taverns: Their History and Laws* (1928)
Batchelor, D. *The English Inn* (1963)
Benham, G. *Inn Signs: Their History and Meaning* (1937)
Burke, T. *The Book of the Inn* (1927); *The English Inn* (1930); *English Inns* (1943)
Cary, J. *Traveller's Companion* (1791)
Day, J. W. *Inns of Sport* (1949)
Delderfield, E. R. *British Inn Signs and their Story* (1965)
Dening, C. F. W. *Old Inns of Bristol* (1943)
Douch, H. L. *Old Cornish Inns* (1966)
Earney, H. W. *Inns of Andover* (1950)
Finn, T. *Pub Games* (1966)
Fothergill, J. *Confessions of an Innkeeper* (1938); *My Three Inns* (1949)
Gadd, W. L. *Great Expectations Country* (1929)
Gaunt, W. *Old Inns of England* (1958)
Hackwood, F. W. *Inns, Ales and Drinking Customs of Old England* (1909)
Harper, G. C. *The Brighton Road* (1892); *The Dover Road* (1895); *The Portsmouth Road* (1895); *The Bath Road* (1899); *The Exeter Road* (1899); *The Norwich Road* (1901); *The Newmarket, Bury, Thetford and Cromer Road* (1904); *The Old Inns of England* 2 volumes (1906); *The Manchester and Glasgow Road* (1907); *Historic and Picturesque Inns of Old England* (1926)
Harrison, B. *Drink and the Victorians: The Temperance Question in England, 1815-72* (1971)

Hogg, G. *Inns and Villages of England* (1966); *A Second Book of Inns and Villages in England* (1967)
Hill, B. *Inn-Signia* (1948)
Hopkins, R. T. *Old English Mills and Inns* (1925); *This London: Its Taverns, Haunts and Memories* (1927)
Keverne, R. *Tales of Old Inns* (1939)
Kitton, F. G. *The Dickens Country* (1905)
Knowles, D. and Hadcock, R. N. *Medieval Religious Houses in England and Wales* (1953)
Larwood, J. and Hotten, J. C. *The History of Signboards from the Earliest Times to the Present Day* (1966) A revised version of this classic book was published in 1951 under the title *English Inn Signs* with an additional chapter by Gerald Millar on later signs.
Long, G. *English Inns and Roadhouses* (1937)
Maskell, H. P. *Taverns of Old England* (1927)
Maskell, H. P. and Gregory, E. W. *Old Country Inns* (1910)
Matz, B. W. *Dickensian Inns and Taverns* (1922); *The Inns and Taverns of Pickwick* (1921)
Monson-Fitzjohn, C. J. *Quaint Signs of Olde Inns* (1926)
Oliver, B. *The Renaissance of the English Public House* (1947)
Popham, H. E. *The Taverns in the Town* (1937)
Rainbird, G. M. *Inns of Kent* (1948)
Richardson, A. E. *The Old Inns of England* (1934)
Richardson, A. E. and Eberlein, H. D. *The English Inn: Past and Present* (1925)
Roper, A. and Boorman, H. R. P. *Kent Inns: A Distillation* (Maidstone 1955)
Shelley, H. C. *Inns and Taverns of Old London* (1923)
Tate, W. E. *Inns and Inn Signs in and near Burton* (1944)
Tristram, W. O. *Coaching Days and Coaching Ways* (1888)
Turner, R. *The Spotted Dog* (1948)
Wagner, L. *London Inns and Taverns* (1924); *More London Inns and Taverns* (1925)
Wakeman, J. *Trust House Britain* (1963)
Watson, R. *A Scrapbook of Inns* (1949)
Wemyss, C. *English Inns Illustrated* (1951)

Wilsman, S. G. *The Black Horsemen: English Inns and King Arthur* (1971)
Yorke, F. W. B. *The Planning and Equipment of Public Houses* (1949)

Acknowledgements

I am greatly indebted to the staff, managers and owners of inns described in this book for their unfailing courtesy in providing me with information and answering my questions. A number of friends have also been extremely helpful; special thanks are due to Mr Robin Gurnett, Mr and Mrs Paul Eldridge, Miss Pauline Hill, Mr J. A. C. Taylor, Mr Vincent Waite and Mrs Joan Whittock.

A. W. COYSH.
October 1971

Index of Inns

Index of People